The Joy of Quilting

by LAURIE SWIM

Introduction by Alex Colville

VIKING

VIKING

Penguin Books Canada Ltd.
    2801 John Street, Markham, Ontario, Canada L3R 1B4
First published by Penguin Books Canada Ltd., 1984

Produced by Harlow Publishing Inc.
    30 Humewood Drive, Toronto, Ontario, Canada M6C 2W4

Canadian Cataloguing in Publication Data

Swim, Laurie.
    The joy of quilting

Bibliography: p.
ISBN 0-670-80050-3

1. Quilting. 1. Title.

TT835.S84 1984   746.46   C84-098632-7

Title Page: **Sugar Plum**
The Artist, 29 x 39 in. (74 x 99 cm)

Photography by Nir Bareket
Book and jacket designed by Ron Kaplansky, R.K. Studios Ltd.
Typesetting by McGill Productions
Color Separation by Bergman Graphics Ltd.
Printed and bound in Canada by The Bryant Press

To the memory
of my dear friends

Sandra MacKenzie
Judith Torno

The sunshine is a glorious birth;
But yet I know, where'er I go,
That there hath passed away a glory
  from the earth.
                    – *Wordsworth*

The Folks
The Artist, 62 x 71 in. (157 x 180 cm)

Acknowledgments

Thanks to Bill and Marie Clarke, Sonny Goldstein, David Kilgour, Victor Levin, Molly Stroyman, Cynthia Good, Ron Lieberman, Torben Petersen, Shirley McManus, Chris Bayliss, Pam Frier, Gail Appel, John Willard, Susan MacDonald, Jean and Doreen. Special thanks to Elizabeth Appel and Rhoda Martin for modelling.

I would also like to thank my parents, Glady and Balfour, for their unfailing encouragement of my brothers Peter and Dan and myself. They always believed in the worth of our work.

And, heartfelt, thank you Larry Goldstein, who initiated this project and brought us all together for it.

Table of Contents

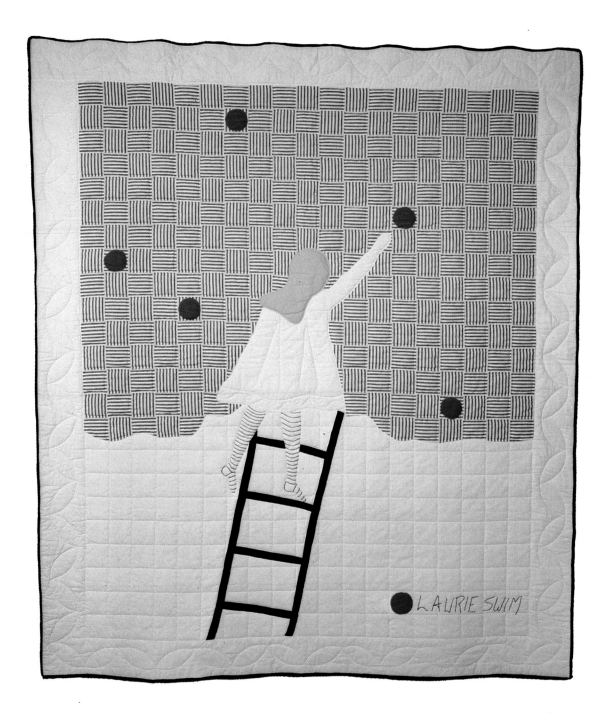

Eve's Apple
Nova Scotia Designer/Craftsman Permanent Collection
62 x 71 in. (234 x 264 cm)

Introduction

I first saw Laurie Swim's work in 1976 when I was a judge at the Nova Scotia Designer Craftsman Exhibition. I have been alive for a long time and I do not have exaggerated expectations; I was astonished and deeply affected when I saw her "Eve's Apple." How can I explain this almost physical response to her work? It is a kind of thrilled cognition, and of course I am not the only one who has experienced it.

Probably one can say that, in our age, we expect the things we use (the products of designers or craftsmen) to be functional and good looking – to be acceptable background material, so to speak. From the so-called fine arts (painting, sculpture, etc.), we expect to be moved – perhaps even seized by the lapels – even though the works may not be very well made. When, without warning, we encounter a utilitarian object like a quilt which also evokes in us a deep emotional response (the kind Panofsky describes as "unspeakable") and when we then, simultaneously, take in the self-effacing craftsmanship of the piece, then we are in the presence of a work of art rare in our time – a quilt by Laurie Swim.

Clearly, I think her work is extraordinarily good. She therefore meets the first requirement that we should make of a person who writes a book on how to do something: the writer must be unquestionably an expert in the field. The second requirement that we should make is that the book be well written – encouraging to the beginner, clear in its explanation of technique, and developed in successive chapters that cover the field in an enlightening way.

People who do something really well are usually good at explaining what they do and how they do it. This is a book by a gifted artist who is also accomplished at telling you how she does it – and how you can do it too.

Alex Colville

Alex Colville, 1984

Preface

If you can sew, you can use this book

The best cooks I know use cookbooks only as a starting point for creating culinary delights. The books may provide the recipes, but the cooks are responsible for the final creations.

For those who know the basics of sewing and have an interest in using that skill creatively, the search for guidance and inspiration beyond simple instruction can pose a delicate problem. To be creative is to explore uncharted waters. That's not hard – it's adventure.

The hard part is taking the first steps.

My purpose in *The Joy of Quilting* is to provide an incentive to the novice as well as to the seasoned quilter and sewer. To those of you who have said, at one time or another, "I want to do something like that someday," I hope to spur you on to making that "someday" today.

Start with a manageable project, one small enough that you can see the end of it, both in size and work-hours. Many projects have been left undone simply because they were too large, too complex, too ambitious.

If your heart is set on a larger work, rather than wait to undertake it, reduce it to a size you can work with – perhaps table-size. On a small scale you can resolve problems that might overwhelm you in a larger format. Besides, smaller works take on a wonderful, precious quality of their own.

Chapter Four of this book is designed to give you a solid grounding in basic techniques. In the sample projects suggested in Chapter Six I started with the simplest and gradually moved to more difficult pieces.

It is up to you to decide whether you use this as a pattern book or as a guide for developing techniques to execute your own ideas. I do, however, encourage you to draw on your own experience and imagination in order to create your individual statements.

There are no hard and fast rules for problem-solving in quilting. We must think in terms of what we can do with a material as well as what has already been done with it. The more experienced sewer may show us the shortest, most obvious way to do something, but the beginner often gives us a fresh approach. Our goal is to strike a balance between the positions, keeping the fresh approach of the novice while always building towards greater technical expertise. As an example, sewing through three layers in even, running stitches gives dimension and life to an otherwise flat surface. It is, however, just one important tool in quilting. Bear in mind that any technique or style which achieves a desired effect can become a working tool for you.

During workshops I have always encouraged the free exchange of ideas. *The Joy of Quilting* is my way of sharing these experiences with you. I hope I will hear from you. Please write to me in care of the publisher – I look forward to the experience!

Laurie Swim

Laurie Swim, July, 1984

St. Michael and the Dragon
Dr. James Nethercott, St. Michael's Hospital, Toronto
27 x 60 in. (69 x 152 cm)

1
THE QUILT

The textile sandwich and its history

"The textile sandwich" is an endearing term describing the four basic elements of the quilt: the backing, the padding, the top, and the stitches that hold it all together. From bread and butter beginnings, the textile sandwich has reached the height of cultural celebration in museums, galleries, private collections and the writings of the critics and experts. The art of quilting has arrived.

The quilted textile has had a long and universal history. Even before the advent of woven cloth, quilting can be imagined as a technique employing animal skins: two layers sewn together with padding between them for greater warmth and strength.

Due to the perishable nature of the materials involved, it is hard to trace the origins of quilting. However, in spite of rot, moths, and wear, there is evidence that quilting provided protection from the cold, the sun, and early armaments in all parts of the world.

The first record of a quilted textile – a carved ivory figure – depicts a Pharaoh of the Egyptian First Dynasty, *circa* 3400 B.C., thought to be wearing a quilted mantle. As well as quilted clothes, there were also mattresses, blankets, rugs, and coverings for door and window openings.

The earliest existing sample of quilting is a carpet believed to have been made sometime between the first century B.C. and the second century A.D. Discovered in 1924 on the floor of a tomb in Mongolia, this piece is amazing for its elaborate figurative detail and a sophisticated design that excites the viewer even to this day. It can be presumed that there was a tradition of this type of work long before this piece was actually made.

Quilting, then, has been with us for thousands of years. Although it did not originate as a decorative art, it has become one in spite of itself. The practical, sometimes rough uses of quilted objects dictated fine workmanship. If the stitches in a garment were not sewn properly, the garment failed. Thus the traditional purposes of quilting distinguish it from other fine needlework. We respect and respond to the natural beauty of it contained within the boundaries of its utilitarianism. The fact that it has aesthetic value is a bonus.

Although quilts and counterpanes existed in Europe, the arrival of settlers in North America marked a new development that expanded the potential of the quilt. It became an important part of daily living and this development has continued to the present.

The first settlers arrived with only the bare essentials to eke out a place for themselves in the new world. They had little to spare and every scrap was used. As clothing wore out and the long-awaited treasured yard goods from overseas were cut up for use, the remnants were carefully saved. The perfect vehicle for their use became the pieced quilt top. The finer pieces were put to a special use. Combined with many loving hands and incredibly long hours of work, appliqué quilts became family heirlooms.

Enough of these homey, lovely creations – both appliqué and pieced quilts – have survived to provide us with a powerful record of their creative and social history. The quilting bee itself became a source of cohesion in the community – a cultural tradition.

It has only been in recent years, however, that these quilts have again been recognized by the general public for the treasures they are. It is part of our heritage to build something from nothing, and we should be proud of that fact.

A new approach to quilting

Quilts have become so popular that it is hard to open any decorator's magazine on sale today without seeing them. It is ironic that it is the modern woman who has reawakened this interest in domestic needlework, not too long ago considered "just women's busywork." Today we are changing our condescending view of this intricate art form. Amish quilts, for example, are as exciting as Mondrian's body of work.

What was regarded as women's work has attracted male enthusiasts as well. Men are not only taking a healthy interest in what is happening in quilting, some, like artist and author Michael James, are participating in opening up new avenues of thought. My point is not that male participation validates the quilt as an art form – it is that all kinds of people are rediscovering an old medium of expression that touches them.

The time is ripe to create tomorrow's heirlooms.

The quilted statement

Wherever and whenever quilts are seen, spoken of or written about – from country fairs to museums to public galleries, from quilters' circles to private collections, from craft publications to *The Sunday New York Times Magazine* – there is a soft-centered sentiment attached, akin to the essence of the quilting medium itself. People everywhere love quilts and quilted things. "The Pleasant Land of Counterpane," a poem by Robert Louis Stevenson, describes a bored child in his sickbed conjuring up a fantasy-land in the hills and valleys of his bed quilt.

In our generation, however, quilts are no longer just counterpanes or bedcovers but have gone on to adorn our walls. This is not to say that all quilts should be hung or that the bed is no longer an honorable place for them. It serves rather to remind us that things of function can be beautiful and can, finally, evolve into pure art.

Because its utilitarian role is becoming less important the quilt can now be regarded as a creative statement. As with painting or other art media, one of the challenges of the art of quilting is to break the barriers of tradition. Paradoxically, another of the challenges of any art is to work within given boundaries to preserve and extend tradition. This, of course, is another facet of quilting.

The world of fabric, tools, and accessories is so readily accessible that you should have no trouble finding materials for your own creations. Selection – both of materials and of techniques – is a kind of freedom: you impose your own restrictions. Innovation and economy are already built into the tradition of quilting and are part of the creative process. It is often the odd-shaped pieces of fabric left over from other works that stir my imagination. I save these pieces down to inches and they usually suggest their own end. What a wonderful feeling I get when a design problem is solved by a scrap of fabric I happened to save.

In addition to a surface image or design, the process of quilting involves the dimension of sculptural relief. Traditionally the hand-quilted

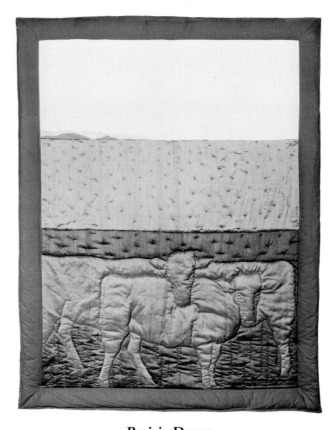

Prairie Dawn
The Bank of Nova Scotia, Lethbridge, 78 x 96 in. (198 x 244 cm)

stitch has been used to hold the textile sandwich together, to keep the batting from shifting, and to fill empty spaces with decoration. Now, however, batting is made of material that holds its shape with minimal quilting, thus giving us more opportunity to manipulate the surface. Although hand-stitching still performs this function, I have always felt that it was too special – as well as time-consuming – to be used only in this way.

In *Prairie Dawn* (above) for instance, I have used hand-stitching specifically to create expression in the faces of the cows: the stitching has no utilitarian function in the construction of the piece.

If, on the other hand, the stitching is more effective hidden, as in the case of an appliquéd shape – around the cows' shapes themselves, for example – I machine-stitch the outline. Not only is it physically stronger, it also emphasizes the embossed effect.

The choice, again, is yours. I feel that hand-quilting is a luxury that you shouldn't hide or over-use. Compared to machine-stitching, the hand-quilted stitch has a more fluid line. Like all things of quality, it should be a show of refined elegance rather than a filler of space.

I have often found it hard to describe what I do. I think of myself as a "quiltist" who prefers to make art. There are artists who sometimes use the quilt as one of their media, even breaking the tradition of cloth and stitching by using plastics, glue, paint, paper – whatever. Yet they somehow retain the concept of "the quilt." And then there are traditional quilters with vision, who, by means of their innate aesthetic sense, carry their work into the realm of art.

There is plenty of room for all of us in the world of quilts. A lot can be learned from our cross-pollination.

Sheep Look Up
David Bayliss, 25 x 34 in. (64 x 86 cm)

2
IMAGERY & INSPIRATION

From the tradition of quilting to individual interpretation

Out of necessity came the quilt and out of the rag bag came its unlimited possibilities. The bed quilt has evolved into an art form – fabric is its medium.

Looking through the work in this book you may conclude that my subjective imagery lends itself mainly to an appliqué technique. I do, however, use all methods of stitchery to enhance the image. These methods include all modes of quiltmaking: piecing, whole cloth, trapunto, as well as embroidery, beading, etc. In other words, I feel free to draw upon whatever tools of stitchery I need to gain the effect I wish to achieve.

My approach to my work is to always start with an image that naturally reflects my mood at the time. Like a painter, I begin with an idea, then go about finding the best way of turning it into a finished piece.

Fabrics and how to collect them

My color palette includes all kinds of fabrics, trims, threads, buttons, and beads. I have collected bags full of rags, and I have an insatiable appetite for rooting through fabric stores, my special favorites being those "hole in the wall," out-of-the-way places that sell odd ends. Often the storekeeper asks, "And what are you going to be using this for?" My reply – "water" or "sky" instead of "lining" or "a dress" – may elicit an odd look from the clerk, but it is a factor in the focusing of my mind on my work. Just as a painter is inspired by oils, fabric evokes a mood in me.

My favorite fabric is silk. It really does have a life of its own. When I look at silk I see the highlights and shadows of our natural surroundings. Nothing about it is flat; color and depth are there in one swatch.

Satins and velvets are a close second choice. Satins are shimmering lights dancing on water; velvets are shadowy depths. These are the Rolls Royces of textiles.

There are many other exciting fabrics, some of which may be even more stirring to your imagination. Quite often materials are made more interesting by their flaws; the dyes in them may have smeared, or prints may have failed to register correctly. These you usually find in the remainder bins, considered junk by others, but you may uncover just the gem you've been looking for to achieve that certain special effect.

And don't stop at the retail fabric stores. Used clothing, drapes from thrift shops, rummage and lawn sales often yield wonderful finds. Old fabrics have a special patina and – as long as they are not rotting – can be used in wall hangings because they are not subjected to the wear and tear a bed quilt has to withstand.

Cynthia's Window
Cynthia Good and Alan Pratt, 80 x 40 in. (203 x 102 cm)

I employ mainly solids in my pieces, using prints only when they are of a nebulous or simple pattern. In one instance, *Two Crows* (page 56), tiny flower patterns became foliage and field. I find in most cases, though, that prints are what they depict – little repeated figures – and are therefore limited in the further uses to which they can be put.

Above all, when looking for fabrics let your imagination take over. This is the stuff from which your creations will grow. Happily, the choice is endless.

The repeated image and the single image

While fabrics may sometimes give you inspiration for images, usually it is the image that determines what is needed in the way of fabric. But if you want to make a wall hanging, don't start by just drawing a picture. First go out and touch some fabrics. Get acquainted. Then come home and sketch.

I begin with a thumb sketch, a drawing a few inches square, to capture my initial idea. This I do in a notebook, making brief notes and leaving space for later additions. Once recorded, these ideas may stay dormant for months or years or forever: they have to be very special in order to make it from paper to a working piece. The thumb sketch records an idea in its simplest form; the bigger the sketch, the greater the embellishment. There is plenty of opportunity for that kind of detail later. The thumb sketch limits me to composition and minimal outline images. If these elements are strong now, the impact of the final piece cannot help but be powerful. The detail is the frosting.

When the time comes I blow up my sketch to the size I want to make the finished piece, usually on a grid. At this point I refine my drawing until it is exactly what I want. Then, using tracing paper, I make patterns of each section I will need. (For a more detailed description, see Chapter Four.)

Some people are unsure of their ability to create and develop original images. If you feel this way I suggest starting with a simple, repeated image.

The repeated image is still, in the tradition of quilt-making as well as in other art media, one of the most powerful methods of design. By taking a single image and repeating it with slight variations in color and position, you can add variety and interest to a piece without losing the impact of the original idea. The pioneer quilters knew this intuitively.

The rule of thumb is: "Simple is best."

If you are at all unsure of your design ability try the following exercise. Draw a simple outline image, make a template of it, and trace it repeatedly, overlapping the images almost at random, on a piece of plain broadcloth. I have found this technique very successful in workshops and have included a similar exercise in Chapter Six (page 58).

When the students finish working on these compositions, quilting them using various colors of thread and/or appliquéing the same image in different fabrics to accent the design, the resulting effect is almost always pleasing and often extraordinary, especially to beginners who thought they could not design their own original pieces.

There have been wonderful groups of cats and baskets of oranges produced from a simple repeated shape. Something I like to suggest is to inject a sense of humor into your work, and the repeated image lends itself to this. After repeating the image a number of times, you get to know it and it may occur to you to make a slight change. One of those cats, for instance, might suddenly peek over the shoulder of another.

One such case in my own work is *Sheep Look Up* (page 16). In the foreground a pair of sheep are nuzzling each other and on the horizon there is one lonely sheep looking up. This piece has always drawn a warm response. The image is a lovable one, very simplified, with small differences making it interesting – a good formula to adhere to.

Another kind of design is a single image that dominates the entire "picture." For examples, look at *Eve's Apple* (page 8), *Two Crows* (page 56), *Nude in the Window* (page 21), and *St. Michael and the Dragon* (page 12), all of which include one simple and all-powerful figure. In each of these the single image is the focal point of the piece, but because I try to keep the image simple, what happens *around* it becomes every bit as important. The stress here is on the overall design rather than just the central image.

Inspiration

When I was seventeen and seeking one correct formula for creativity, I met an experienced artist – a painter and sculptor – and asked him about inspiration. He patiently explained to me that if I were to wait for it, and if I were lucky, inspiration would come to me perhaps once a year, like a birthday cake. Sometimes we are lucky, but most of the time we have to work like beavers while waiting, learning to make it happen.

At seventeen, I thought that growing up as I did, in a small fishing village in Nova Scotia, without any formal art training, was a limitation. Only years later, after studying at art schools, teaching, traveling, and working on my own did I realize that my first loves, the sea and quilting, were my strongest sources of inspiration and therefore the natural direction I should take. An old, obvious truth, perhaps, but one never arrived at easily.

Always do what you know first. The rest will follow. *Seascape* (page 20), for instance, came into being shortly after I had settled in Toronto. There was a call for an entry in an exhibition entitled "Inside Nova Scotia." The problem presented was to create a fiber piece for an architectural space. I chose to create something for a waiting area, the kind of place in which you find yourself with little to do but read old magazines and daydream – hotel lobbies, doctors' and lawyers' offices, etc. If I found myself in such a situation, what would my fantasy be? It would probably revolve around images of the sea; a serene sea set in a mood of mystery would pass time very nicely. Let the viewer in the waiting area, I thought, make up his or her own reverie and nourish the imagination rather than dwell on the frustration of a forced break in a heavy schedule. City people, I had noticed, are almost always in a rush.

Seascape
Moe and Minda Davis, 48 in. Diam. (122 cm diam.)

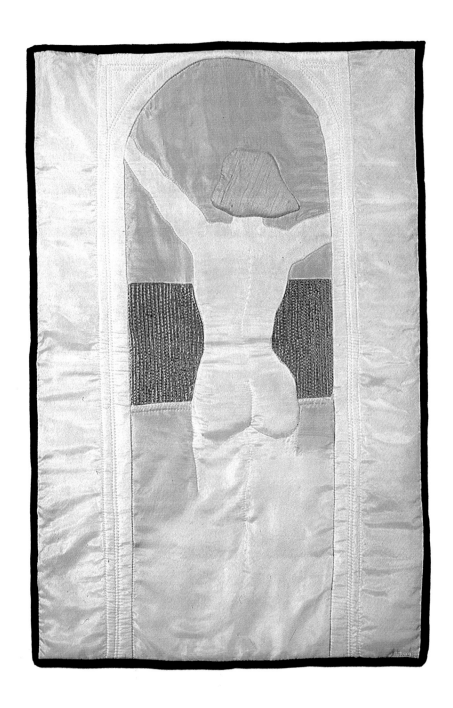

Nude in Window
Private Collection, 40 x 60 in. (102 x 152 cm)

Seascape in Location

With all this in mind I sat down with paper and colored pencils and set about designing the piece. I decided to use a circle to distance the viewer from the traditional rectangular format of the bed quilt. The circle also conjured up the idea of looking through a telescope, which is often associated with the sea. I then broke up my circle with three planes of contrasting textures representing sand, sea, and sky.

I did the sand in rough linen, the sea in quilted blue satin, and the sky in the same satin overlaid with sheer white silk. Repeating the circle motif in the form of an umbrella on the beach provided the piece with both its focal point and a sense of mystery.

Once I started working on the design in fabric, I began to make exciting discoveries. The satin, broken up by quilted stitching, caught the shimmering light and shadow of water; depending on changing light conditions during the day, it changed shade just as the sea does. The overlay of thin white silk on the same satin produced a translucent sky.

I love this piece, not only because the finished work pleases me but because every aspect of its development was satisfying – the circumstances, the inspiration, the design process, the contrasting fabric textures, and the unexpected effects I discovered along the way.

This work also marked my final realization that quilting can be an art form. Apart from the fact that it was made of quilted fabric, it bore no relation to a functional bed quilt. And it met the criteria of the architects who sponsored the exhibit: it was chosen as one of the entries.

The point of this story is that you will find your inspiration in the world around you and the feelings and the ideas it evokes in you. Observe everyday objects, scenes, and moods that interest or move you. You don't even have to leave home to do this. Look out the window and then look away. What is left is an imprint on the mind. That impression, not a literal interpretation, is what should be used to start working.

Light up the mundane with your own intelligence, your own imagination, and give it new life. Work ideas into simple, manageable shapes and arrange them in a form that pleases you. Inspiration is really an attitude. It's that simple.

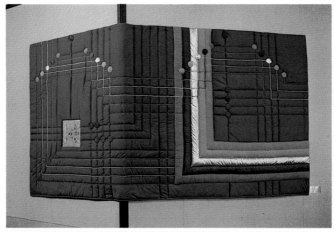

Circuity, *Hudson's Bay Company,* 10 x 5 ft. (3.04 x 1.52 m)

Equinox, *The Bank of Nova Scotia, Toronto,* 64 x 4 ft. (19.5 x 1.2 m)

Cognizance,*Ryder Machinery, Toronto,* 14 x 6 ft. (12.7 x 1.8 m)

3
QUILTED WALL HANGINGS

Adapting the quilt to design criteria

Quilted wall hangings are "soft murals." They enhance their environs with physical and visual warmth, just as tapestries did long ago in medieval castles. They soften the sounds, tensions, and hard edges of modern structures. Their humanizing presence is making them more and more popular with both private and corporate collectors.

Whether a quilted piece is found hanging in a home or in a corporate space, it seems to become the center of attention. Color, shape, and texture play a part in this, but it is also the elevation of common fabric – that which we wear and use daily – to the realm of visual art that draws our immediate interest.

Paintings are not meant to be touched. They remain apart from us. The textures of soft wall murals draw us closer. We want to touch them, and that feeling blesses them with serenity.

I have often been called upon to design a piece for a given space. Sometimes my client has particular needs that I must fill or problems that must be solved, and this adds to the challenge. It is like listening to a story and imagining the pictures to go with it.

Although it is unlikely that you will find yourself designing a piece for an abattoir or a forklift machinery rental company (*Cognizance*, page 24), you can benefit by drawing on the interest or hobbies of family and friends for inspiration in your own work. Combining different elements from several

sources can give expression to whimsy.

Designing for a space does not mean dealing with just a blank wall; it also means observing the space around it and objects already in the room. As I mentioned before, the quilted mural will most likely be the focal point of a space without even trying to compete, so if you take into account other already-existing elements they can enhance your work. For examples, look at the grid ceiling of the building in which *Equinox* (page 24) hangs or the horseshoe mahogany receptionist's desk which is echoed in the bottom curve of *Cognizance*.

Methods of hanging

The method of hanging a work can make or break the way we view it as a whole and is therefore an all-important decision in finishing any piece.

Sewing a sleeve along the top and inserting a wooden rod will support light-weight pieces evenly, and screw eyes can be attached to each end of the rod for hanging. If you break the sleeve into three sections and leave two gaps

Diagram 1: *Sleeve with openings for hanging piece.*

between them (see Diagram 1), the piece can also be hung from the two openings in the fabric. Adding another sleeve and rod along the bottom of the wall hanging will weigh it down if necessary.

Smaller pieces do not always need a rod to support them; two or three rings sewn to the top may be sufficient. I have found that small metal washers are best for this: they do not break, fit neatly at corners, and are less apt to show after the piece has hung for a while. Sewing each ring in two places distributes the weight and minimizes pulling of the material when hung (see Diagram 2).

Diagram 2: *Sew washer or ring in two places.*

Velcro® is another good material to use for hanging. The soft side of the Velcro® is sewn to the quilt, and the stiff looped half can be stapled to a wooden bar or attached directly to the wall with a staple gun. This is especially handy for free-shaped pieces like *Cognizance* (page 24), *Seascape* (page 20), and *St. Michael and the Dragon* (page 12). In each of these a Velcro® support strip was placed in the upper middle half of the piece and several tabs were attached at different points to secure it.

Also, if there are discrepancies in the border because the fabric has stretched, as it sometimes does when sewn, the Velcro® allows you to ease and adjust the material of the hanging into a smooth line. Velcro®, being related to fabric, is a natural for hanging pieces. When in place the work hugs the wall in a snug way, and it can be removed easily for cleaning and maintenance.

There are many other methods to consider when it comes to attaching your piece of work to a wall. I've used right-angled screw-in hooks, round-headed screws, and even cup-hooks. You can fit a wooden rod into a cup-hook, which is tidy and neat. Remember to use plugs in a plaster wall.

If you are hesitant about putting holes in the wall, suspending a piece from the moulding with a nylon filament like fishing line is a good alternative. This also frees you, if you have a selection of them, to change your wall hangings periodically.

How to add support

To prevent a piece from sagging make a stretcher to support it. I did this for *Sea Brides* (page 28) and for *Boats on Blue* (page 45). Sew a 4 inch (10 cm) wide sleeve to each of the four sides of the piece, making each a few inches short of the corners. Then take four flat pieces of finished cured wood moulding approximately 3 inches (8 cm) wide, and insert them into the sleeves. Pull the piece out to its longest extension with the wood in place. (This is definitely a two-person job.) Clamp where the corners meet at right angles (see Diagram 3). Hold the piece up and check the tension of the front of it, adjusting if needed. Mark and number corners. Remove clamps. Cut the wood to length, drill holes for ¼ inch (6 mm) stove bolts, reinsert into sleeves, and fasten with wing nuts. Hang from corners.

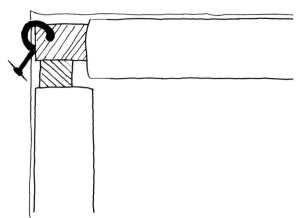

Diagram 3: *Flat wood pieces in fabric sleeves with clamped corner.*

Another technique for adding support and body is to back a piece with a slab of flexible polyurethane foam, as I did with *Sugar Plum* (page 92). Cut the foam to size. Sew a wide binding to the front of your piece (approximately 3 inches (8 cm) for a 1 inch (2.5 cm) foam slab). Place the piece face down and lay the foam over it. Fold the binding over the foam. Pin and baste the binding material to the foam. Measure and cut the backing material, leaving an allowance for folding the four sides under. Press. Finally, sew the backing material to the binding material. For an accent, I sometimes sew a cord or insert piping to the edge of the front border. The value of foam is that, especially with a smaller piece, it adds body and density without making the work rigid. As a hanging apparatus, use rings or washers.

How to care for a quilted wall hanging

Most quilted pieces can be maintained by vacuuming lightly above the surface without actually touching it. An alternative is to attach with safety pins a light-weight fabric or a piece of screening to the surface and vacuum with an upholstery attachment.

Every six months or so it is advisable to take the piece from the wall, lay it face down on a sheet on the floor, and vacuum from behind to prevent dust from settling in.

As a precautionary measure you may want to spray Scotchguard® over the surface soon after completion. This helps prevent stains from those fingers that can't keep away from your work, but it should, however, be tested on scraps of fabrics used in the piece before you risk applying it to the finished work.

At some point – hopefully not for years to come – you may have to have your work cleaned. If dry cleaning is necessary, make sure that it is done by someone who specializes in delicate fabrics. A good way to find such a specialist is to call your local museum and ask the person who deals with the care of their textiles.

If you have a piece with a white background that needs cleaning you may have to wash it by hand (dry cleaning sometimes tends to yellow white fabric). Fold the quilt accordian-style and immerse it in the bathtub with warm water and a mild soap. Let the water out without removing the quilt. Fill the tub with warm water again, then empty it. Repeat the process until the water remains clear. Press out the water carefully.

Hand-washing is best done in warm weather since a good way to dry a quilt is to place it face down on a clean sheet outside on the grass.

Should you have to store your piece, cover the top with tissue paper and loosely roll it up. Do not put it in a plastic bag, as sealed-up humidity may cause damage. Storing in a cedar chest is certainly the best method, but an appropriately-sized box or drawer will do, along with a few mothballs wrapped in a scrap of fabric.

If you treat your creations with care – the less handling the better – they should endure for many years.

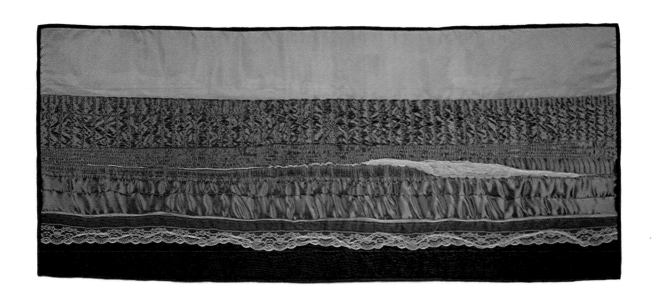

Sea Brides
The Artist, 80 x 36 in. (203 x 91 cm)

4
THE FABRIC MEDIUM

Traditional methods
and innovative techniques

True creativity requires the ability to execute an original thought. Just as a seed will soon die if it is not watered, so a good idea will wither away if it is not nourished with a knowledge of processes and their practical applications.

This chapter contains technical information that will enable you to create your own pictorial fabric art. In Chapter Six, where I give step-by-step instructions for the designs I am sharing with you, I will refer back to the methods of achieving certain effects described in this chapter.

I do not, however, want you to feel limited to one technique in executing my designs. In some instances I offer several solutions to the same problem, leaving you free to choose the one that best suits your style. I suggest that you read through this chapter *twice*; first to acquaint yourself with terminology and ideas, then once again to clarify the processes I describe.

By becoming familiar with more recently developed techniques as well as traditional methods I hope you will acquire a broad general knowledge of the fabric medium, and will feel comfortable not only in following my instructions in Chapter Six but also in developing your own ideas and designs.

The surface design from paper to fabric

#1 The working drawing
Preparing an idea or a design for your fabric piece requires careful planning. It is at this stage that you make your most important decisions and find out how it will all go together in the end.

If you are starting with a thumb sketch as I suggested in Chapter Two, now is the time to refine and enlarge it. Retaining the simplicity of your smaller sketch, lay out your design on a piece of card paper at least 9 x 12 inches (23 x 30 cm) or larger if you prefer. Use round numbers for the dimensions so that it will be easier to scale up to the finished size at later stages.

For example, if you intend your finished piece to be 3 x 4 feet (.91 x 1.2 m), I suggest that the dimensions of the drawing should be 6 x 8 inches (15 x 20 cm) so that the scale of the enlargement will be two inches to the foot (or 1 cm to 6 cm). The idea is to choose measurements which will allow you to enlarge the sketch without complicated calculations.

If you are starting with a photograph, a magazine picture or a montage (a picture made by superimposing or combining a number of different pictorial elements), prepare your working drawing by tracing simple outline shapes of the original pieces onto paper.

After finishing your design in pencil, retrace the lines with a fine felt-tipped pen to produce a sharper outline and then erase any trace of the pencil markings. This will give you a good, clean, sharp image, a working drawing with which to proceed.

#2 Enlarging the working drawing

The easiest ways to enlarge or reduce a design are to make a photostat to the exact size, or to use an overhead projector which may be borrowed from a school, library or business. Unfortunately these methods may not be convenient or readily available. Unless you feel confident that you can enlarge the design freehand, the most reliable and practical method is the grid.

Step 1. Superimpose a grid on the design you wish to enlarge, drawing it either on the design itself, or on a sheet of tracing paper which you can lay on top of the design (see Diagram 1, Figure i). The size of the squares will depend on the size of the design. Use ⅛ inch (3 mm) squares for smaller designs; ¼, ½, 1 or 2 inch (6, 12, 25 or 50 mm) squares for larger pieces.

In the designs illustrated in Chapter Six, this step is predetermined for you, with the grid guide framing the design. All you have to do to make the grid is place a sheet of tracing paper over the design and join the lines with a ruler.

Step 2. Decide what each square in your grid represents in the final size of your piece. For example, if you wish to make your piece four times as large as the drawing you are working from, each square in your final design will have to become four times larger. If each square on your working drawing is ¼ inch (6 mm), that

Diagram 1

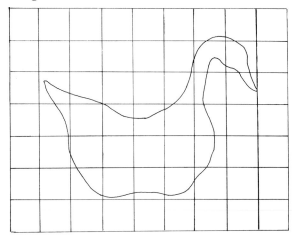

Figure i: *Grid superimposed on original sketch.*

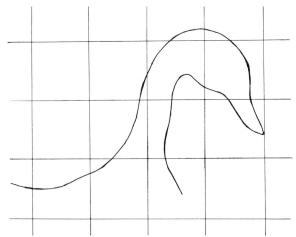

Figure ii: *Grid squares are four times larger than in Figure i. Shape is drawn square by square to duplicate original design.*

square multiplied by four becomes 1 inch (2.5 cm) in the blow-up of your design (see Diagram 1, Figure ii).

Step 3. Now that you have determined the scale, draw the larger squares on a piece of paper the same size as your final design. Then copy the design freehand, square by square.

It may not be necessary to copy a whole design. For example where there is one main figure, as in *Eve's Apple* (see page 74), it is necessary to grid and copy only the figure of the girl, not the entire quilt.

A dressmaker's layout board with various sizes of grids already marked out on it saves a step. If you are using one, just lay tracing paper on the board, choose the grid size you want, and draw the image on the tracing paper.

If you are drawing your own grid, I suggest that you work on tough brown wrapping paper: it's a good, sturdy working material and is available in large sizes. Measure off the squares in pencil. After filling in your drawing, retrace the outline with a felt-tipped pen to sharpen it and to distinguish it from the grid.

#3 Pattern-making

Now that you have a finished enlargement of your design plan there are several possible ways of transferring the design to fabric. You will be the judge of what best suits your needs. Most of these methods can be used either for transferring guidelines for quilting or in preparation of appliqué pieces.

Using the drawing as a pattern

The following three techniques, used directly with the large paper drawing of your design, are best for simple shapes.

Carbon paper. One way to transfer lines to the background or appliqué material is to place dressmaker's carbon paper between the drawing and the fabric, pin them together, and carefully trace the outline with a dry ballpoint pen or a dressmaker's tracing wheel. This is best suited to smaller shapes as large sheets of carbon paper are not readily available.

Perforated patterns. Perforate the line drawing first with a tracing wheel, place it over the fabric, then dust or draw over the perforated lines with chalk. Chalk works well if you want to leave a light, temporary line on the fabric; it rubs off easily. If you want a more permanent line for quilting or cutting out a shape, use a hard lead pencil instead to go over the perforations – dark for light-colored fabrics, a white tailor's pencil for darker ones.

Templates. If you cut out the shapes of your design and use them as patterns to trace out your shapes on the fabric, you have what are called templates. It is a good idea to number the pieces on the right side so that you know which side is up and how the pieces go back together again. It is also important that the paper used

for the templates be heavy enough to withstand tracing around the edges.

For more intricate designs I generally prefer to leave my drawing untouched as a guide for placement of my pattern pieces on the background. I make tracing paper copies of the original and use them as my patterns. That way, if I make a mistake I can go back to the original and make another copy. The following are methods to use with tracing paper patterns.

Using tracing paper patterns to transfer guidelines

Carbon paper. Again, I use dressmaker's carbon paper, but this time the way it is used in dressmaking – with a translucent paper pattern. First you tape the fabric to a table or the floor, depending on size. Pin the tracing paper with your design on it to each corner of the fabric. This will give you a secure base from which to work, limiting movement of both fabric and paper. Slip a strip of carbon paper between the layers and carefully trace the lines on the tracing paper, moving the carbon paper as you go. Presto! Your drawing is on the fabric.

Lead pencil. Turn over your tracing paper pattern and with a soft, thick lead pencil retrace the lines on the reverse side of the transparent drawing. Place the pattern right side up on the fabric and secure it with pins. Retrace the lines with a blunt stylus or an empty ballpoint pen. The pencilled line will be transferred to the fabric.

These two methods are terrific for filling in details inside your shapes as well as outlining the main form. See also *Stitched guideline using tracing paper* (page 35).

The appliqué

Before you experiment with more innovative techniques you should get to know the traditional methods. This will enable you to weigh the advantages of both.

Traditional methods of appliqué

Basic. The oldest method for making the appliqué is to cut the shape out of the fabric, leaving a seam allowance of 1/8 to 1/4 inches (3 to 6 mm) all around it. Notches should be cut in the seam allowance to make smooth curves and sharp points possible (see Diagram 2).

Caledon Hills
Mr. and Mrs. J.D. Creighton, 48 x 84 in. (122 x 213 cm).

Redhead
Barry Torno, 27 x 46 in. (69 x 117 cm)

On an outward curve, cut small notches or wedges from the seam allowance at regular intervals. On an inward curve, clip into the seam allowance at regular intervals; the sharper the curve, the closer the intervals. Be careful not to cut past the seamline. Trim the seam allowance only where you need to reduce bulk. At corners and points, trim across close to the seam and then diagonally from the point on either side (see Diagram 2).

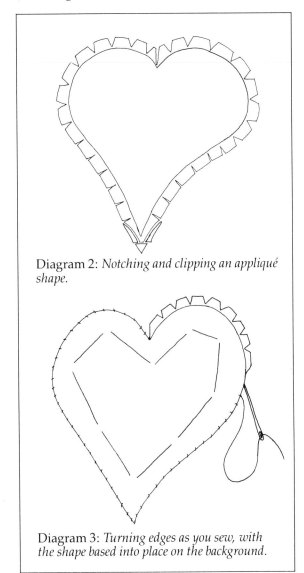

Diagram 2: *Notching and clipping an appliqué shape.*

Diagram 3: *Turning edges as you sew, with the shape based into place on the background.*

Once you have cut out, notched, and trimmed your appliqué, you can either turn the edge under and baste or baste the shape direct-ly to the background fabric, then turn the edges under as you sew it permanently in place (see Diagram 3). This method is best used only with natural fabrics because they are less apt to fray. It takes an experienced hand to achieve a smooth and well-defined line while sewing fine stitches.

English appliqué. This technique is easier to control. First make a cardboard template, trace as many shapes as are needed onto newsprint or magazine paper, then cut them out. Reverse each shape, unless it is symmetrical, and pin it to the wrong side of your fabric. Cut the shape out of the fabric, leaving an edge allowance of $\frac{1}{8}$ to $\frac{1}{4}$ inches (3 to 6 mm). After notching the edges as needed, turn them under and baste, using the paper as your guide (see Diagram 4). Start appliquéing the shape to your background fabric, leaving an opening just large enough to allow removal of the paper. Remove the basting, then complete sewing.

A variation is to leave the paper in place in order to reinforce the shape. A modern version of this idea is to use interfacing instead of paper. Iron-on interfacing gives even better control.

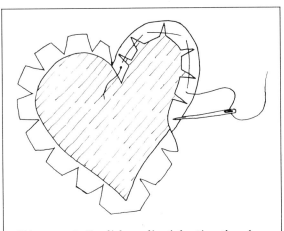

Diagram 4: *English appliqué: basting the edges with the paper in place.*

Stitched guideline. After drawing the shape on the fabric, sew by machine, following the line (see Diagram 5). This helps prevent the fabric from fraying, as well as giving you a defined line at which to turn your edge. This technique is especially useful when working with fragile fabrics such as silk, velvet, and satin.

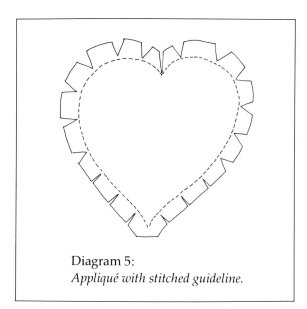

Diagram 5:
Appliqué with stitched guideline.

Stitched guideline using tracing paper. A variation is to draw the shape first on tracing paper instead of on fabric, and then sew the paper to the fabric by machine. This is my favorite method because I find it easier to follow complex lines and maintain accuracy; the paper also helps to hold the fabric straight. When the sewing is finished, tear away the paper. There's a trick to this. Take hold of the outside edge of the paper and pull it towards the sewn line, so that it tears cleanly along the line of stitches. The paper inside the sewn line should then come away cleanly, in one piece. Now trim the shape leaving ⅛ to ¼ inches (3 to 6 mm) allowance.

Non-traditional appliqué techniques

I am certain there is nothing new on earth, just variations on established themes. I have devised some variations for my own appliqué work through the natural course of discovery and experience. My aim has always been to achieve a simple and expedient way of appliquéing that also suited my work.

Quite a while ago I was trying to create a curved line and had problems both with fraying of the fabric and a lack of definition in the finished line. I decided that *facing* the shaped line was the logical thing to do, just as it is in making clothing. In following this train of thought I worked out the following methods.

The faced appliqué. The advantage of facing the appliqué is that you have a finished shape to work with at a stage when it is important to concentrate fully on sewing a fine stitch. It frees you from having to deal with raw edges, thus allowing you to handle more intricate shapes.

Start with two layers of fabric instead of one. Lay down right side up the material you wish to appear in the finished piece, then lay the facing material on top of it. Transfer the outline of the shape, without reversing the pattern, to the upper surface. Sew the two pieces together along the outline, then trim, notch, and clip the usual seam allowance. Now, pull the two sides away from each other and make a slit in the facing fabric, just large enough for your fingers to turn the shape inside out (see Diagram 6).

Diagram 6: *Faced appliqué technique. The upper fabric, with the slit, is the facing material. The shaded fabric will become the front of the shape when the appliqué is turned inside out.*

After turning it inside out, push a blunt stylus or pointer (a flat wooden tool made for this job) through the opening to define sharp points or corners your fingers can't get into (see Diagram 7). If some points are too tiny even for the stylus, carefully pull the fabric out to its finished shape from the outside with a needle (see Diagram 8).

Dampen and press with an iron, using a pointer from the inside or a needle from the outside to fill out the shape of the seam.

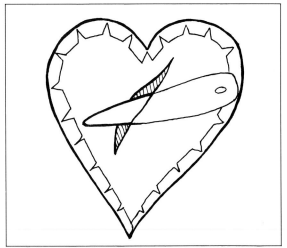

Diagram 7: *Faced appliqué technique. An X-ray view, showing how a pointer can be used to push the seams into place through the slit in the facing.*

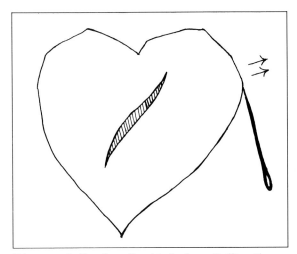

Diagram 8: *Faced appliqué technique. Pulling the seam out with a needle before pressing the appliqueé.*

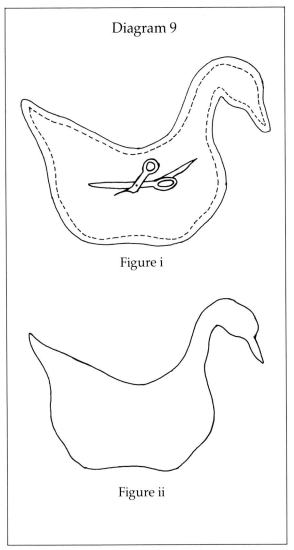

When the shape is asymmetrical the faced side in which the cut is made (Figure i) shows the true image (Figure ii).

You now have a well-defined and finished-edge appliqué to work with.

If you find that the double thickness of your appliqué presents a problem, trim your facing to within about ½ inch (12 mm) of your seamed outline to get rid of the bulk.

When working with an asymmetrical shape, it is sometimes hard to tell which is the right side to cut for turning inside out. Remember that, in the raw state, the true image appears on the side of the facing, the side in which you will make the slit (see Diagram 9).

You may also want to try the following variations for special effect.

For *accent and contrast* try facing your image with a different colored fabric than the front; it gives an outline to the image, visually a nice touch.

For *economy* you may choose to use a cheaper or lighter fabric for the facing material; after all, the facing is virtually invisible, and could be a waste of expensive fabric. For example, you can face a piece of silk with broadcloth of the same hue; or if your main concern is to save weight, use colored interfacing.

Cockatoo
George Biggar and Mary Cornish
48 x 60 in. (122 x 152 cm)

For *accentuated bas relief,* you can insert batting into a faced appliqué. I do this in two ways. The simpler method is to place a layer of batting underneath the two layers of fabric, then sew the three layers together in one step (see Diagram 10). Now trim, cut, and turn inside out as usual. If there are detail lines to be quilted they can be done before sewing the appliqué to the background. For an example of this technique, look at the instructions for *Sheep Look Up* (page 71).

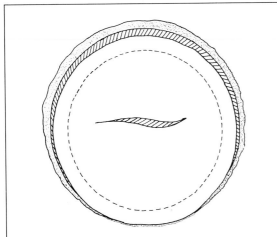

Diagram 10: *To make a padded faced appliqué, sew the two layers of fabric to a bottom layer of batting.*

For *prominent bas relief,* pin the fabric on which your final image will appear to an underlayer of batting. Then transfer your pattern onto the fabric and sew the two layers together following the outline of the image. You can now, if you wish, draw in the inside detail lines. Trim off the excess batting as close as you can to the sewn line, but do *not* trim the fabric (see Diagram 11).

Lay the fabric face down on your facing material, pin and baste. Using the stitched outline of your image on the batting side as a guide, machine-sew another line approximately ⅛ inch (3 mm) outside the image line. If you require more depth, sew further away from the image line. After trimming and making a slit in the facing material, turn inside out as before. When you appliqué this to your background you will have a prominent bas relief.

Diagram 11

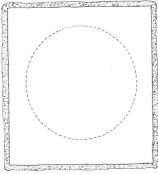

Figure i

To add extra dimension to a shaped appliqué, first sew a piece of fabric to a piece of batting, along the outline of your shape.

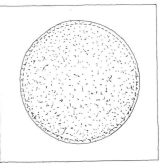

Figure ii

Reverse and trim the batting, but not the fabric.

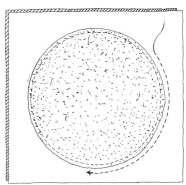

Figure iii

Place on top of a second piece of fabric, and sew together outside the first row of stitches. Trim and turn inside out for prominent bas relief.

Machine appliqué. Any of the turned-edge appliqués described in this chapter can be applied to surfaces using a sewing machine, either with straight or zig-zag stitching. However, if you are using a raw-edge appliqué (a fabric shape with no edge allowance for turning) with satin stitch on your machine, here are a few tips to help you maintain better control.

The most successful satin-stitched appliqué has a narrow crisp line of stitching around it. I find a lot of machine appliqués disappointing on close inspection because the edges are ragged and the lines out of control. A patient hand and lots of practice are needed for success in machine appliqué. You must also have, of course, a good machine with a fine satin stitch.

The biggest problems with this type of appliqué lie in keeping the raw edges from fraying and avoiding movement or puckering of the fabric as it is sewn down. In dealing with small pieces use fusible webbing that bonds when placed between two layers of fabric; it minimizes fraying of the edges. For larger shapes, lining with an iron-on interfacing will give added support to the fabric and its raw edge, as it does in the English appliqué. Just remember to cut the shape with the webbing or interfacing at one and the same time.

Careful basting to the background material with either hand or machine-stitching is absolutely necessary to maintain control. Hand-guide your appliqué without pushing or pulling the fabric under the needle, and when you are finished thread a needle and use it to pull the threads to the back.

Machine appliqué can be very effective. Try using its linear outlines to advantage, and experiment with contrasting threads for accentuation.

The backing

The quilt backing can be made of any soft fabric that the needle will glide through easily. Natural fabrics are the best for this; blends are stiffer and tend not to mold so well to the quilting. Although the choice is usually natural unbleached cotton or muslin, any color or print can be used.

In the past, used flour sacks were opened and pieced together to make backings. You may find you still have to sew together yardage in strips to cover a large area. You can also use one large piece of sheeting as long as it is all cotton or cotton-like.

Most quilters, as a matter of pride, try to make the back of a piece look as good as the front. Very often the back, when quilted, has a charm of its own not unlike that of a whole cloth quilt (a quilt top made with only one piece of fabric).

In my pictorial work I very often find myself using two layers of backing, one for working and a final one for show. For instance, if I am working with a design I have divided into smaller sections to be pieced together later, or if I have opened up the back to add or remove stuffing for effect, I might add a new backing material, tacking it to the first backing if necessary before binding its edges.

The batting

Batting is the filler, the middle layer that when stitched produces the lovely bas relief for which the quilt is known.

In the past people used what was available as filler. Sometimes this was even an old blanket, but more likely it was a cotton or wool batt. The cotton batt has definite limitations in that if it is not closely quilted – that is, in areas of no more than 2 x 2 inches (5 x 5 cm) – it shifts and lumps with washing and wear. The wool batt has the springiness of modern polyester plus added warmth, and it does keep its shape, but it is not so easy to find. Therefore the freely available dacron and polyester batts are really most suitable for our needs. They come in various widths and thicknesses, and they are easy to handle and clean. To avoid tiny fibers poking through the surface of your quilt, giving it a woolly appearance, buy a glazed or bonded batt. You should find the finishing process marked on the label of the package.

An alternative to batting is Insulite®, a heavy polyester felt used as interlining in clothing and for quilting and other crafts. For surface texture, it is flatter and tighter in appearance. In wall hangings, for instance,

Sheep on a Hillside
Mr. and Mrs. Walter Gordon, 72 x 39 in. (183 x 99 cm)

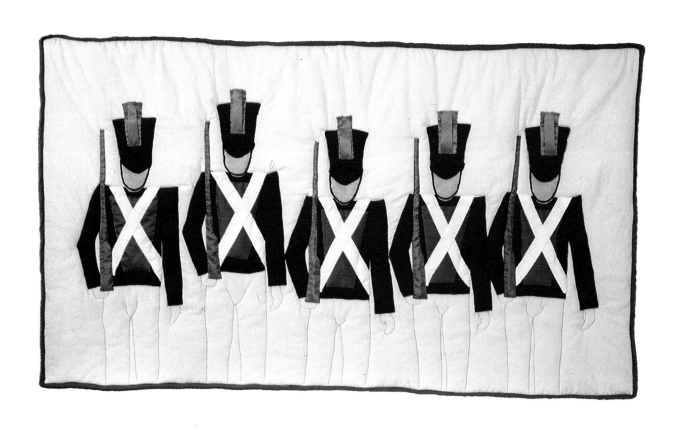

Soldiers
The Artist, 64 x 36 in. (163 x 91 cm)

there may be areas you want to be flatter than others. For examples, see *Twofold* (page 48), *Sea Brides* (page 28), *Caledon Hills* (page 32), and *Nude in Window* (page 21). It is also used for the placemats, bib, potholder and child's vest in Chapters Five and Six.

Making a textile sandwich

Traditionally the three layers of the quilt were brought together in a large quilter's frame the size of the piece. The frame consisted of four separate bars of wood held together at the corners, which meant that while it was being made the quilt occupied a lot of space. Because this is impractical for most of us, we are more inclined to do the quilting in a smaller frame, in a hoop or on a table surface.

Start by stretching your backing, seam side up, on a large flat surface. For the largest pieces be prepared to use the floor. Fix the backing to the surface at intervals with masking tape. Lay the batting carefully on the backing. Now put down the top, smoothing out any unevenness, and fasten with straight pins. Then, starting in the middle and working outward (see Diagram 12), baste stitches no smaller than 3 inches (8 cm) towards each corner of your piece. Baste from the center to the middle of each side. Now baste concentric squares with lines 8 to 10 inches (20 to 25 cm) apart, finishing with a row of stitches to secure the edge.

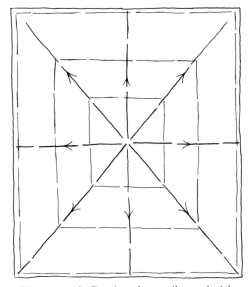

Diagram 12: *Basting the textile sandwich.*

The three layers can now be placed tautly in a hoop or frame for quilting. For working on small pieces approximately 30 x 40 inches (76 x 102 cm) or less, I use a canvas stretcher from a local art store. These stretchers come with sides in standard lengths, so you can assemble the size you require. Buy the sides about 4 inches (10 cm) larger than the size of the piece you are working on. Then, using a heavy strong thread, lace the piece to the frame. Alternatively you can use a frame approximately the same size as the piece, and secure it with pushpins. In both cases start stretching in the middle of each side and work out towards the corners. The advantage of using a frame is that you can see your overall design better than with a hoop.

A quilting hoop about 23 inches (58 cm) in diameter is more practical than traditional quilting bars for larger work because it is portable. You start by placing the center of your piece in the hoop, and then you work out from there concentrically. Make sure you pull the fabric layers evenly in all directions before proceeding with the quilting. When you come to the corners or sides of the piece, add muslin strips to fill the empty section of the hoop so that it has something to grip.

A table surface is most likely used only in special cases. In *Sheep Look Up* (Page 16) I wanted to create an uneven surface in contrast to the generally smooth surface achieved by stretching the work. If you want this kind of texture in only one part of your design, start out on the table surface and then put the piece in a frame or a hoop to finish off the smooth areas.

The quilting

The hand-quilt stitch is a series of neat, even running stitches, the needle piercing through the surface layer, the batt, and the backing, then up to the surface again. With practice you should be able to pick up two to four stitches at a time (see Diagram 13).

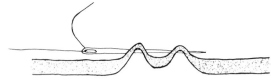

Diagram 13: *The quilting stitch.*

It is the quilting that sets off the quilted piece. It adds dimension and texture to an otherwise flat surface.

Some diligent quilters aim for 12 stitches per inch (5 per cm). The results of this industrious undertaking are amazing to look at. You may enjoy setting yourself the challenge, but it isn't really necessary. A seasoned quilter explained it to me in this way: if you sew less than 6 stitches per inch (2.5 per cm) the stress is on the thread rather than being evenly spread between thread and fabric. You are also less able to control the neatness of your stitch. On the other hand, if your stitches are tiny and close together the stress is on the fabric, which with time may actually tear. The target is a happy medium of between 7 and 9 stitches per inch (3 and 3.5 per cm). This, too, will vary with the demands of the material used. In other words, don't be too hard on yourself as long as you can manage a neat, even stitch. That is what is really important in hand work.

You should use a quilting needle, short and slender, designed to pick up the tiny, even stitches required. Most quilters find they can work better with a thimble.

If you are a beginner at quilting I recommend that you practice before you start your first large piece so that your stitches don't change as you progress. You will be surprised how quickly you can gain proficiency through practice. Go slowly at first until you find the rhythm. It will become a soothing and relaxing pastime.

For appliqué, quilting around the shape may well be enough. If your design has large empty background areas, however, you may want to embellish them with quilting. For straight lines, as in the white area of *Eve's Apple* (page 8), you can use masking tape as a guide, carefully pulling away the tape after you have finished.

When using a template for a quilt guideline I try whenever I can to avoid drawing around the shape with a pencil. For simple shapes I use straight pins. After placing the template on the surface fabric, I outline the shape by putting in a line of straight pins at right angles to the surface. This is how the eggs were quilted in

The French Hen (page 81). I remove the pins as I quilt up to them.

A pencil outline leaves marks in the fabric. If, however, you find it necessary to use a pencil for an intricate shape, use a number 3 or 4 hard lead instead of a common HB or softer lead. Make the lightest of lines. If you are using a perforated pattern, the hard lead will leave the tiniest dotted line as your guide.

Machine-quilting. Your choice of hand or machine-quilting should be based on personal preference and the design of your piece. If it is a sharply defined line you are looking for, a machine-stitched indentation will provide it. It is stronger physically as well as visually. For an example of how both hand and machine-quilting can be used together, look at *Sea Brides* (page 28); this work depends on line to distinguish and enhance its texture.

The single major disadvantage of machine-quilting is the limitation in the size of the piece imposed by the arm of your machine. Avoiding this problem takes planning. You can roll up the piece or divide your work into smaller, more manageable sections to be sewn together later. In either case the layers should be well secured with basting beforehand to prevent them from shifting.

You should always try to start machine-quilting in the center of your piece and move out, as recommended in hand-quilting. Adjust the tension on your machine to accept several layers and set the machine to make 12 to 14 stitches per inch.

Lower the needle into the fabric and proceed without backtracking, leaving loose threads to be woven into the back later. To sew around curves and corners, leave the needle in the fabric, raise the pressure foot, move the fabric into position, then proceed.

Embossing. Machine-sewing has been used to enhance the design in *Soldiers* (page 41) and in the tea cosy *Basket of Eggs* (page 66). In these I used the machine as a drawing tool to define the legs (*Soldiers*) and the eggs (*Basket of Eggs*); I also used it to emboss the appliquéd shapes by sewing as closely as possible around them. The line of stitches buries itself in the fabric,

His Pride
Edie and Sonny Goldstein, 64 x 58 in. (163 x 147 cm)

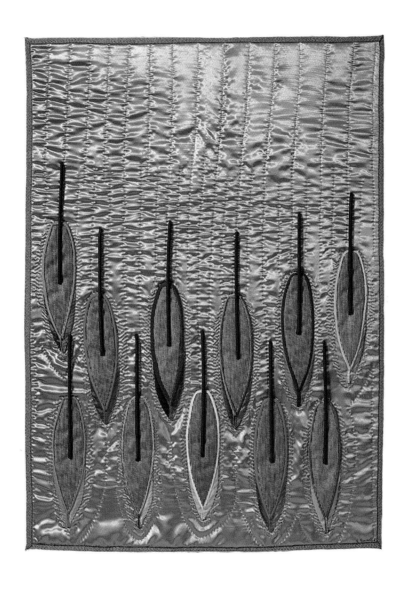

Boats on Blue
Elaine and Stephen Dewar, 27 x 38 in. (69 x 97 cm)

and the shape literally pops out. This can be done by hand but the effect is more marked when the machine is used.

Invisible strip quilting. When strips of fabric are used in a design, your stitching can be made invisible. For an exaggerated example of this technique, look at *Equinox* (page 24), a major architectural installation. In this piece I used strip quilting to arrive at a tubular effect. Another example is *Cognizance* (page 24).

Start with a layer of batting and backing. Lay down your first strip and attach the next strip to it by placing it on top of the first with edges touching. Sew the seam on your machine. Fold back the second strip and continue with the next one in the same way. Or you can sew your strips together first and then sew them seam by seam to the batting and backing. Whichever way you choose, you will have neat, clean indentations on the surface without visible stitching (see Diagram 14).

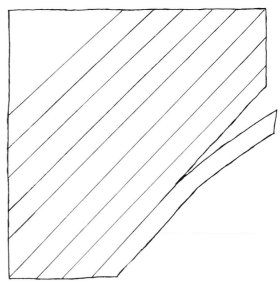

Diagram 15: *Cutting guidelines for bias binding.*

From this center line mark out the parallel lines in the widths required. Use a yardstick and a pencil to draw guidelines for cutting. Cut out the strips and sew the diagonal ends together to make one continuous length (see Diagram 16). Remember to make all your seams on the same side of the strips.

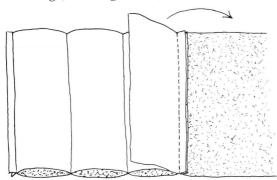

Diagram 14: *Invisible strip quilting.*

The binding

The binding usually consists of fabric cut into approximately 1½ inch (4 cm) wide strips. It is a good idea to iron a folded seam allowance along each edge of the strip, then fold it in half and press it lengthwise once again. The pressed folds will guide you in your sewing.

The strips can be cut either on the bias or on the straight grain of the fabric. If you choose the bias method, first fold your fabric diagonally, cross-grain of the fabric. Finger press or iron to obtain a creased line as your guide (see Diagram 15).

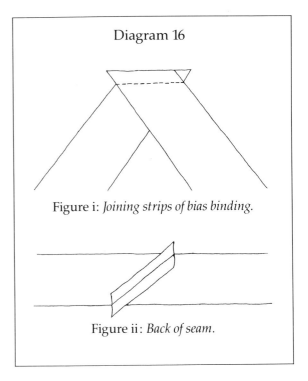

Diagram 16

Figure i: *Joining strips of bias binding.*

Figure ii: *Back of seam.*

For binding cut from the straight grain of the fabric, you require a length of material a little in excess of the longest side of the finished piece to provide enough to finish the corners neatly and properly. Using a yardstick, mark out four strips, one for each side.

If you are binding with bias strip, you have the choice of either cutting a strip for each side of the piece or using one long continuous strip to go all the way around the work. If you cut a strip for each side – either bias or straight grain – work one pair of opposite sides first, then the other pair.

I can suggest two ways of sewing on the binding. Each starts with pinning and basting the binding to the piece. If you prefer hand-finishing, sew the binding by hand or by machine to the front of the piece, then fold the fabric around to the back. Secure it with pins, and hand-sew with a blindstitch.

Your binding can also be finished entirely on the machine. Start this time by sewing the strip to the back of the piece. Fold to the front, baste, and machine-sew a line as close to the inside edge as possible.

It is important that the corners of the piece be neatly finished. The simplest method is to fold the end of your binding around the back and finish by hand.

Mitering the corners is, however, more attractive. To start and finish the binding, see Diagram 18, fig. i-iv. To miter a corner using a continuous bias binding, referring to Diagram 17 sew almost to the edge, then backtrack a few stitches (Step 1). Make a right-angle fold in the binding strip, line it up with the next edge, and keep on sewing (Step 2). Repeat this procedure at each corner. Wrap the binding strip round to the other side of the piece (Step 3). Then hand- or machine-stitch the other edge of the binding strip in place, making a right-angle fold at each corner (Step 4).

If you are using four separate strips to bind your piece, sew on the first pair of sides, then as you sew on the second pair sew them only up to the inside corner. Leave excess fabric to be folded at an angle to the outside corner, and around to the back of the piece (see Diagram 18).

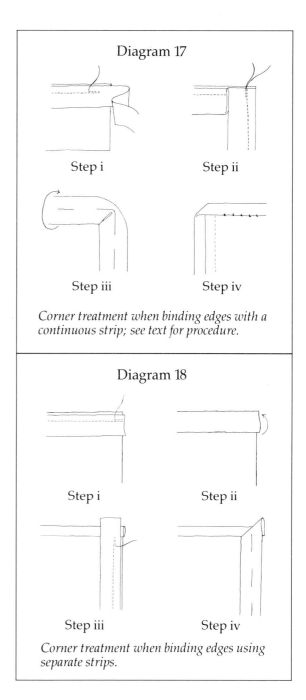

Diagram 17

Step i   Step ii

Step iii   Step iv

Corner treatment when binding edges with a continuous strip; see text for procedure.

Diagram 18

Step i   Step ii

Step iii   Step iv

Corner treatment when binding edges using separate strips.

Special Effects

Sometimes a work in progress requires something special to make it take off, a twist to turn it into an individual statement. Some solutions may be unorthodox while others are developments of techniques used in needle-work since its beginnings. In any case it is important to have a broad knowledge of

Twofold
Cathy Lace and Hugh Mackenzie, 45 x 92 in. (114 x 234 cm)

Cut from the Same Cloth
The Artist, 52 x 42 in. (132 x 107 cm)

needlework of all kinds to call upon. If you can't see how you can use this knowledge to resolve a problem, you can strike out on your own. You can break with tradition and look at your work with a fresh eye. Ask yourself what will make the piece work and then experiment, however outlandishly, because some of the unlikeliest ideas may lead you to a resolution. The following techniques were discovered largely by accident.

To interpret water in such pieces as *Seascape* (page 20), *Boats on Blue* (page 45), *Nude in Window* (page 21), *Twofold* (page 48), and *Sea Brides* (page 28), I broke up the plain blue satin surface with rows of vertical stitching to create the dips you find in an open body of water. With the light of the passing day these pieces actually turn different shades of blue, much like real water.

As I mentioned earlier the stitching was done by hand, not in a frame but on a table top. Using a strong thread and holding it taut after every couple of stitches I used my fingers to manipulate the surface, gathering and flattening the satin as I went along. If you use this technique remember to secure the thread firmly at the beginning and end of every row.

For interpreting sky and other soft effects I use overlays of sheer silk, the type used in making silk scarves. It allows for subtly changing colors; the translucent quality adds depth. The simplest examples are in the skies in *Seascape* (page 20) and *Nude in Window* (page 21).

I also used this method in *Nude in Window* to define the figure inside the balcony. Specifically, I sandwiched a beige fabric between the silk and the padding to create the shadow.

I did much the same in *Sea Brides* (page 28). To provide a gradation between the horizon and the upper sky, as well as a hint of clouds, I placed sheer pink nylon, the type used in lingerie, between the silk and satin of the sky.

In *Twofold* (page 48), I wanted to capture the dawning or fading of daylight, the time all animals come for their feeding. I used the pink nylon again for clouds on top of a bright yellow cotton base overlaid with a pink silk.

When using this type of sheer silk you have to be careful not to snag it with rough finger-nails, dull needles or pins. If a crease needs pressing try a dry iron at a low temperature first, and if that doesn't work wet the silk completely and press dry with a steam iron.

The dress in *Sugar Plum* (page 92) is made of sheer blue organza on top of a background of muted blue cotton. This was done to distinguish the dress from the background by changing its texture.

To make a shape more conspicuous put in extra padding. If you have not done it prior to appliquéing the shape to the background, it is perfectly legitimate to slit a small opening in the backing under the quilted shape and push in a suitable amount of stuffing to make it more pronounced. Sometimes you may find that a shape is too prominent, in which case you can take out a piece of batting. After slitting the backing use a small pair of scissors to carefully clip away excess stuffing. This is where you might consider using a second backing to cover and tidy the reverse side of your piece.

Shirring is formed by stitching and gathering several rows in the fabric. You can make as many rows as you wish. The best fabrics to work with are soft and lightweight. I used this textural technique for the clowns in *Rain or Shine* (page 51) and for the bodies of the sheep in *Sheep* (page 40) and *Twofold* (page 48).

Use a strong thread in your bobbin so that it won't snap when you gather the fabric. Knot by hand both ends of each row of gathering. To achieve the appliqué shape, first face the shape (method on page 35), placing the stitching guideline on the facing fabric. Machine-sew the shape with small stitches to secure the shirring. Cut out the shape. Slit the facing and turn inside out. This is a wonderful way to create a textural shape. Note that in *Rain or Shine* I have used many colorful cottons to create the clown outfits.

Trapunto or corded quilting is traditionally a set of parallel lines of stitching through which strands of yarn or cord are drawn with a large needle called a bodkin. The bodkin is threaded through from the back, through small slits cut at intervals in the fabric. I used this technique for the beach in *Sea Brides*

Rain or Shine
M. Charlebois, 52 x 45 in. (132 x 114 cm)

(page 28). As you can see, it accentuates the lines.

Reverse appliqué is a process in which a shape is cut out of the ground fabric and another fabric applied underneath. This technique is widely used in Central and South America and in Hawaii; it is an interesting way to create a negative rather than a positive shape.

For a variation of this technique refer to *Eve's Apple* (page 8), *Two Crows* (page 56), and *Nude in Window* (page 21). In all these pieces the colored areas are negative shapes cut out and placed on a neutral white background. In each case the figure is defined by what is around it, the fabric of the figure being part of the ground fabric.

For small detailed accents and touches I have used embroidery, trims, buttons, and beads. In very special cases, such as the shadow on a cheekbone, I have sparingly colored with crayon, then ironed the fabric through a piece of cotton to absorb the wax and blend it with the background.

As you become more experienced and confident you will likely find new techniques of your own. The message here is that anything goes as long as it works.

Landscape, 18 x 12 in. (46 x 30 cm)

The Calico Gingerbread Man, 15 in. (38 cm)

The Raggedy Man, 15 in. (38 cm)

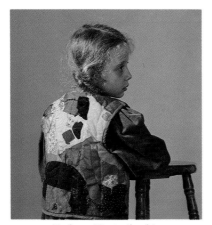

Bolero Vest, *(back)*

Bolero Vest, *(front)*

5
PLAYTIME

Creating with scraps
for the child in all of us

Here are a few simple projects both for you and for the children in your life. If you don't have a child of your own, borrow one. Children are great for inspiration, pushing and freeing your imagination into play time. Work along with them and see the creations grow. Most of all, have fun.

Landscape
Photo on page 52.

The fabric sketch on page opposite is approximately 18 x 12 inches (46 x 30 cm) actual size, a good average size for this kind of work. Start by taping a backing fabric larger than the proposed finished work to a flat surface. Pin or baste a layer of batting to the backing. Cut out a middle ground to extend from the horizon line (the bottom of the tree line) to the bottom of the piece. In this sketch I used the different colors of thread in the fabric to advantage by cutting it on the bias in order to represent the long field grass. Place the fabric on the batting surface. All of the fabric shapes are cut to the size needed, with no seam allowance, showing a raw edge.

For the sky I used a strip of blue satin. For the trees I dug into my scrap bag and picked out all the greens I could find, in various shades, prints, and textures. When you have assembled your fabrics, use your scissors like a draw-

ing tool, cutting the shapes freehand. Let your hand guide you rather than just your eye; the shapes will come naturally. When you think you have cut enough shapes, start arranging them on a strip of iron-on interfacing, adhesive side up. When the strip is covered and you have an arrangement that pleases you, press the pieces into place with an iron. Trim excess interfacing from the shape. For extra security place a piece of dark netting on top and place the whole section on the background to meet the field and the sky. Baste in place.

For the foreground I cut out several pieces of floral print and overlapped them to create dimension. Also, using the scissors to draw, I cut out different shaped strips of green. When everything was in place I machine-quilted in and around the shapes to bring them to life. The netting on the trees was trimmed and a few lines of quilting, as well as beads, were added to the middle ground. The piece was trimmed, bound, and stretched on a canvas stretcher.

Bolero Vest
Photo on page 52.

Children love to show off what they have created and what better way to give them this kind of well-earned satisfaction than with this wearable vest, which can also express a child's individuality. You may find yourself at the end of a production line if they decide these vests could be great gifts for friends! They're a wonderful rainy day project.

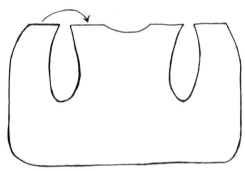

Bolero vest pattern

The Bolero. Make a paper pattern out of newspaper following the illustration of the vest pattern shown here. Fit it to the child, making adjustments as necessary in the length and in the armholes, making sure to leave excess at the shoulders, for seam allowance and for final adjustments.

Lay the pattern flat on a piece of white polyester felt (Insulite®) and cut out. Place the felt on a flat surface. Now provide the child with plenty of scraps, a pair of scissors, and these ground rules: total freedom in choice of colors, textures, and shapes *but* the entire area of felt must be covered. No white must show, even at the edges of the vest. Overlap will be trimmed off later. All of the fabric pieces are raw edge.

When the child has finished, place netting over the entire shape while it is still on the flat surface. Use pins initially to hold it all together, then baste all over. (Your child may be able to do this.) When everything is secure, place the whole piece on a layer of lining material and machine sew the outline of the vest. Trim the netting, the lining, and any overlapping fabric from outside the outline.

A child who can use a sewing machine should be able to put in the horizontal and vertical quilting lines which hold all the layers together.

Now remove the basting. To finish, bind all round with bias trim. For final fitting, try it on the child and make necessary adjustments at the shoulders, pinning the seams on the outside. Sew the shoulder seams out, trim, and cover with a strip of binding. Top stitch.

The Calico Gingerbread Man
Photo on page 52.

This is a doll for an infant, a soft brightly-colored toy with a simple recognizable shape and features. It can be made by an older child for a new baby out of strips of bright colors and prints. The finished size is 15 inches (38 cm) high.

Method. Start by enlarging the simple cookie-cutter shape on this page. One square in the diagram = 2 inches (5 cm) in the final piece. Cut the shape out of paper for use as a pattern.

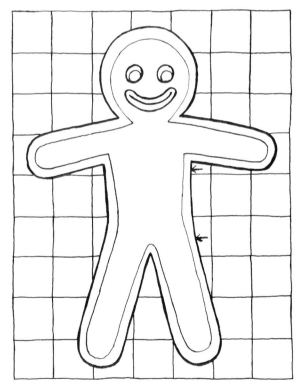

Pattern for The Calico Gingerbread Man

Cut or tear strips out of leftover fabrics. Make into 18 inch (46 cm) vertical strips for the length of the doll and join enough together, sewing them by machine, to make approximately 25 inches (64 cm) width of material. Shirr the fabric (page 50) by sewing horizontal lines 1¾ inches (44 mm) apart across the strips of fabric. Use strong thread in your sewing machine to do this. Separating the bobbin thread from the top thread, hold in one hand while gathering the material with the other. Do this with each row of stitching until the width of your material has been reduced to about 16 inches (41 cm).

Draw out the shape of the doll on another piece of fabric 16 x 18 inches (41 x 46 cm). Lay this, drawing side up, on top of the gathered fabric, which should be right side up. Sew on the machine, following the drawn outline. Trim the shape and turn inside out (see instructions for Faced Appliqué, page 35).

Draw the doll shape again, this time on two layers of fabric. Sew together and turn.

Place the two shapes together with the pieced shape facing out and sew them together following the inside guideline shown in the illustration, approximately ½ inch (13 mm) inside the shape. Leave an opening on one side from the underarm to halfway down the leg. Stuff the body and close up the side seam.

Cut the eyes and the mouth from felt, and secure them to the face by sewing with embroidery floss. A word of caution: don't use buttons for eyes, because an infant may chew them off and swallow them.

The Raggedy Man
Photo on page 52.

This was a project I undertook with multiply handicapped children. Among their problems were poor hand/eye co-ordination, and limited attention span. The success of these figurines lies in the easy manipulation of bright colored pieces of fabric. It is a project for all ages.

Method. You will need two coat hangers, pliers, and wire clippers for making the armature. Open one hanger, bend one end for the head, make a bend for the end of the leg, one at the crotch, one at the end of the other leg, and fold back the wire to the crotch, trimming any surplus there. From the second hanger, cut a double length for the arms. Start by twisting one end around the neck, make one arm length then double back, make another fold at the end of the second arm and fold back to the neck. If the armature seems wobbly at this point don't worry, we're about to fix it. Take a length of nylon stocking and knot it under the arms. Cross over and around the base of the arms and torso and continue wrapping around the head and the rest of the arms. Knot another piece of stocking to the torso and wrap the rest of the torso and the legs.

Cut and tear fabrics into strips 1½ inches (38 mm) wide and about 8 inches (20 cm) long. Tie the strips close together, covering the figurine until it is complete. Fold the ends of the legs to make feet. For hair, knot yarn to the wire loop which forms the head. The results can be delightful.

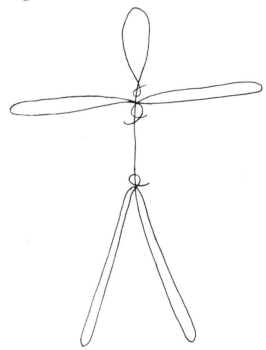

Armature for The Raggedy Man

Two Crows
McCall's Craft and Needlework Magazine
45 x 72 in. (114 x 183 cm)

6
PROJECTS

Projects – Step-by-step instructions

Each quilted piece we make is practice for the next one. Remembering this, our minds stay open to the flow of new information, always improving our experience from one adventure to the next.

Beginning with easier exercises and proceeding to more ambitious projects, I hope to cover here most of the techniques described in Chapter Four and at the same time build up your experience so that you feel confident about creating your own designs. I encourage you to take liberties with the projects that follow, taking what you need and adding something of your own to make them completely yours. And, of course, feel free to use your own favorite colors, patterns, and fabrics if you prefer them to mine.

Materials and tools

First, there are standard materials to keep in stock. The beauty of the quilting medium is that you probably already have most of these materials on hand or readily available. I have suggested alternatives in case you have difficulty finding some items. This is only a general checklist for reference, and you should decide what you need for each individual project before making a purchase. As you broaden the scope of your work you will probably find it desirable to invest in a wider selection of tools.

Scissors. It is important to have a pair which is used solely for cutting fabric. A good pair

is a worthwhile investment, because it is probably your single most important tool. When shopping for this item, it may be a good idea to take along different fabrics to test the versatility of the scissors. Pay special attention to the points, which you will need for snipping into hard-to-get-at places. You should also have a pair of scissors for cutting paper, and a pair of embroidery snips for trimming threads.

Rulers and other measuring devices. A measuring tape is a basic necessity for sewing. You should also have a yardstick (meterstick) for marking or lining up straight edges. A metal one is best as it does not warp and gives a hard edge to work against when making straight lines. A set-square or tee-square is a must for lining up and finishing corners. It is also a good idea to have on hand a smaller ruler of 12 or 18 inches (30-46 cm) as well as an item which you will find very useful, a dressmaker's gauge – a tiny ruler with an adjustable marker for transferring smaller measurements such as seam allowances.

Needles and pins. Keep a good selection of needles on hand. Sharps are the most common and probably the most important. They are long enough and slender enough for use with most fabrics. You will also need quilting needles, often referred to as "Shorts", for making the small even stitches required in quilting. A few embroidery needles, a bodkin, and a darning needle are useful at times and should also be kept on hand. Don't forget straight pins; keep long and short sizes ready for use.

Threads. I recommend that you buy threads to suit the fabrics you intend to use; cotton for cottons, polyester blends for cotton polyester, etc. I keep on hand at all times large spools of black, white, and neutral grey. In addition to these I keep a spool each of red, yellow, green, and several shades of blue (there seem to be so many blues!). This selection should cover most situations but when buying fabric for a specific project it's advisable to match the thread at the same time. There is nothing more frustrating than finding part way through a project that you are without the correct thread. It's also a good idea to keep a range of embroidery flosses for accenting certain lines, and for signing your piece.

Frames and hoops. Traditionally quilter's bars are used for large quilted pieces. I have not mentioned them in my instructions because they need so much space, but if you happen to have a set, by all means use them when working on large pieces.

A quilting hoop about 23 inches (58 cm) in diameter is, however, easier to come by and more manageable for both large and small work.

I also mentioned in Chapter Four (page 42) that canvas stretchers can be used in much the same way as quilter's bars. They are good for medium sized works, and their advantage is that they enable you to see the whole design as it progresses.

Paper. For scaling up a design and making patterns and templates which are only going to be used a few times you can use brown wrapping paper. It is best to buy it by the roll so that you will have a large, clean surface on which to work. Your local butcher or grocer may be able to supply you with lengths cut from bulk rolls.

More important, especially for my methods, is tracing paper. I recommend buying this by the roll because it comes approxi-

mately 40 inches (1 m) wide, matching the width of most fabrics. You cut off the length needed for each project, of course. Rolls can be bought from art supply stores, and in addition to being more useful are more economical than buying by the sheet.

An alternative to tracing paper is tissue paper which is easily acquired. It is large enough for small projects and sheets can be taped together for larger ones.

In addition you will probably require card and construction paper, and cardboard for templates that have to be used repeatedly. Heavy clear plastic sheet is also useful for templates that receive heavy wear.

Pencils and other markers. You should have hard and soft lead pencils as well as tailor's chalk and tailor's pencils; also carbon paper and a dressmaker's tracing wheel or a dry ballpoint pen. Fine felt-tipped pens are useful for sharpening lines in your designs and patterns.

In addition. Build up a collection of buttons, beads, trims, and ribbons. You can buy them as they are needed or do as I do and rummage through the odds and ends bins in fabric stores. These notions are nice to have at hand, even in small quantities. They are part of your palette and sometimes suggest things to you just by being there.

SMALL, MANAGEABLE, AND PRACTICAL
Oranges, Apples, Bananas, and Pears

Four placemats using fruit as a design motif.
Photos on page 60.

This project involves simple shapes that illustrate how easy it is to design by repeating shapes to make a pleasant composition. It will also take you through the process of making a faced appliqué and using machine-quilting as a drawing tool.

Fruit placements. Each placemat is regular size – about 20 x 13 inches (51 x 33 cm).

Suggested materials. Cotton or cotton-like fabrics are used in the images, tops and backing. For padding I use Insulite®, a heavy polyester felt, but you can use regular batting

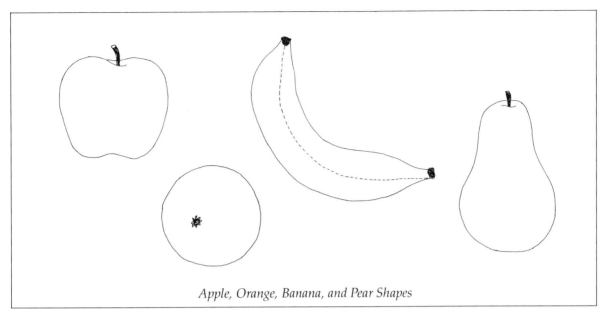

Apple, Orange, Banana, and Pear Shapes

if you wish. The accents are done in embroidery floss, and the stitching in contrasting and matching thread. Pre-wash all fabrics.

You will also need card paper for a template or pattern of the fruit; a sheet of paper 22 x 15 inches (56 x 38 cm) for the drawing; tracing or tissue paper for transferring the design to the fabric; and a soft lead pencil or dressmaker's carbon.

Method. Draw a single life-size fruit on a piece of card paper. Cut out the shape. On a sheet of paper approximately 22 x 15 inches (56 x 38 cm) draw the oval shape of the placemat. Use an existing placemat, if you have one, as a pattern. Starting in the center of the design, trace your first shape using the cut-out fruit as a pattern. Repeat this procedure, overlapping the shapes until you have a composition that pleases you.

Place tracing paper on top of your design and retrace the composition. Turn the tracing paper over and retrace the lines in soft lead (unless you have chosen to use carbon paper) to transfer the design to the fabric. For description of the methods, see page 31.

For the appliqué place the traced drawing on top of two layers of the fabric you have chosen (with carbon in between paper and fabric if you are using it). Go over the outline of the overall shape (the inside lines come later) with a dry ballpoint pen to transfer the line onto the fabric. Sew together, following the outline, on the machine. Trim shape ¼ inch (6 mm) all round. Notch and clip (page 34). Make a slit in the side on which the true image appears, and turn inside out (page 35). Dampen, pushing seams out, and press (page 35, 36).

Fit your tracing paper drawing on top of the appliqué again and transfer the inside lines in the same way as you did the outline. Set to one side.

Make the placemat form by cutting the shape from the original drawing or use an existing placemat as a pattern. Beginning with the backing, then a layer of padding, then the face fabric, place your pattern on top and trace around it. Sew the three layers together on the machine. Trim the shape. Transfer the quilting lines from the pattern to the placemat using tracing paper or carbon paper. In the photos you will see that I have treated the backgrounds in different ways.

Place your appliqué of fruit on the placemat. Baste the inside of the shape, as well as the outline (diagram page 42). On the machine, start quilting the shapes from the center and work out concentrically. Do the outline of the overall shape last. Remove basting. Bind the placemat with bias binding (page 46). Add accents with embroidery floss.

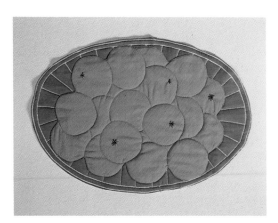

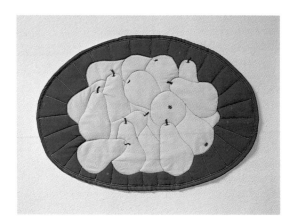

Fruit Placemats

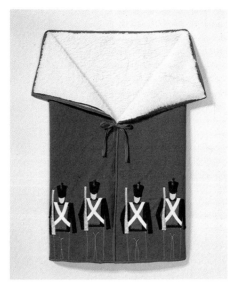

Soldiers Baby Bunting

A Basket of Eggs Tea Cosy

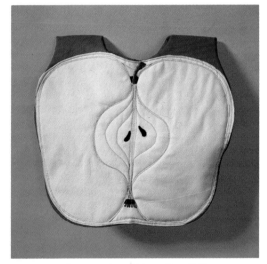

The Apple of Your Eye Bib

A Slice of Cucumber and The Apple of Your Eye

Potholder and bib
Photos on pages 62 and 61.

These two small projects use cross-sections of cucumbers and apples as a source of design. Other naturals would be oranges, pears, watermelons, tomatoes, peppers, and artichokes, to name just a few.

A Slice of Cucumber. The finished size is approximately 12 inches (30 cm) in diameter. This is a two-handed potholder.

Suggested materials. Cotton or cotton-like fabrics are used. You will need a 14 inch (36 cm) square of white for the background. For the backing and bias binding trim use a ½ yard (46 cm) of bottle green. For the light green center appliqué, use two pieces of fabric 7 x 7 inches (18 cm). For the padding use either polyester felt or batting. For thread, use light and dark green. You will also need paper for the drawing; tracing or tissue paper for doing the appliqué; and a soft lead pencil or dressmaker's carbon.

Method. Draw a circle 12 inches (30 cm) in diameter on your paper. Following the illustration, draw in details of the center (the easiest way is to start by dividing the center into three

sections and then fill in the lines). In the illustration, dark lines represent the fabric outlines and lighter lines are the machine stitching.

Make a tracing of the central appliqué, including inside lines. Transfer just the outline of the appliqué to two layers of light green fabric either with soft pencil or dressmaker's carbon, as in the placemat project or see page 31. Sew the appliqué on the machine, trim, notch and clip the shape (page 34). Slit and turn it inside out (page 35). Dampen, push seams outward, and press (page 35, 36). Transfer the rest of the drawing from the tracing to the front of the appliqué the same way as you did the outline.

Make the potholder form by first cutting the circle from the original drawing. Place it on top of the white fabric and draw around it. Sew the white background to a layer of padding and green backing. Trim the shape.

Baste the appliqué in place. Sew the outline of the appliqué, plus inside lines, in light and dark green thread. Sew with light green outside the appliqué, adding the rounded corners to the three seed sections, and add a wavy outline around the outside edge of the potholder.

Bind with green bias binding (page 46). Before finishing the binding, insert a loop made from binding strip for hanging the potholder.

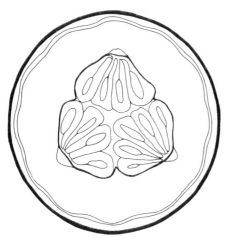

A Slice of Cucumber Pattern

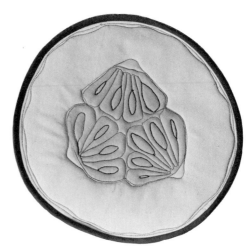

A Slice of Cucumber

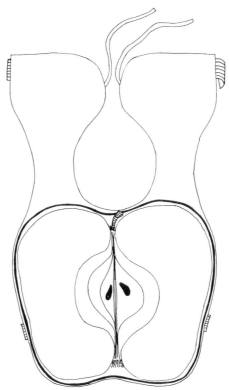

The Apple of Your Eye, Apple Appliqué and Bib Pattern

The Apple of Your Eye. The finished size of this piece depends on the size of the child you are making the bib for. The apple appliqué of the bib shown here is intended to be approximately 12 inches (30 cm) square.

Suggested materials. Cotton or cotton-like fabrics are used. You will need two 14 inch (36 cm) squares of white unbleached cotton for the apple slice. For the bib form, you will need 1 yard (91 cm) of red fabric. For the padding, use either polyester felt or batting the size of the bib form. You will need red and green thread and black and brown embroidery floss. To attach the back to the front under the arm, you will need 8 inches (20 cm) of elastic.

You will also need paper at least 28 x 16 inches (71 x 41 cm) for the drawing; tracing or tissue paper for the appliqué; and a soft lead pencil or dressmaker's carbon.

Method. Draw the apple shape on paper, adding inside details. Fill in the lines for the rest of the bib as shown in the illustration. Dark lines are the fabric shape and fine lines represent the lines of stitching.

Make a traced drawing of the apple. Transfer just the outline of the apple to the two layers of white fabric either with soft lead pencil or with dressmaker's carbon, as in the preceding two projects. Sew on the machine, trim, notch and clip the shape (page 34). Slit and turn inside out (page 35). Dampen, push the seams outwards, and press (page 35, 36). Transfer the rest of the drawing to the front of the appliqué in the same way as the outline.

Make the bib, first cutting out the shape from the drawing, altering the size if necessary to fit the child. Place it on top of two layers of red fabric and trace around it. Machine-sew the two layers of red to a layer of polyester felt or batting underneath them, following the outline. Leave an opening at the bottom of the front of the bib. Trim the shape, notch and clip (page 34). Use the opening to turn the shape inside out, then sew up the opening.

Baste the appliqué in place. Sew the outline of the apple, and machine-quilt the inside lines. Embroider the stem, the seeds, and the bottom of the core.

Sew ties onto the back flaps and attach the front to the back with lengths of elastic.

63

The Pillow Cat

The Pillow Cat and A Basket of Eggs

Cushion and tea-cosy
Photos on pages 64 and 61.

The designs of these two projects relate to the three-dimensional shapes they will become in their finished forms. Here we will create the magic of illusion.

The Pillow Cat. The finished size of this piece is approximately 14 x 13 inches (36 x 33 cm) – but make it larger if you prefer. One square in the diagram = 4 inches (10 cm) in the finished piece.

Suggested materials. The pillow is made of cotton or cotton-like fabrics. You need ¾ yard (69 cm) of dark grey fabric for the front and back of the cushion. For white areas and the stuffed cushion form, you need ¾ yard (69 cm) of unbleached cotton. For padding the front you

need a piece of polyester batting the size of the body, and another piece for the head. For the cushion, you need pillow stuffing. For thread, you need dark grey and white, and you need brown and black embroidery floss for eyes and nose. A draw-string is also needed to close the back of the cushion top.

You also require drawing paper at least 16 x 15 inches (41 x 38 cm), and tracing or tissue paper for making the appliqué patterns.

Method. Make a tracing of the cat in the illustration, joining the lines on the grid surrounding it. On paper draw a grid in 4 inch (10 cm) squares, and fill in the drawing, referring to the tracing. The thick lines represent the appliqués, the broken line indicates where the appliqué pieces overlap. Thin lines represent quilting. When completed, make tracings for patterns of the three white areas and the head.

The Pillow Cat, 1 square = 4 inches (10 cm)

To make the white areas sew each pattern to two layers of fabric. Remove the paper (page 35). Trim, notch, and clip shapes (page 34). Slit the side on which the true image appears (page 35), and turn inside out. Dampen and push out seams (page 34, 35); press. To make the head, sew tracing paper to two layers of grey fabric, adding a bottom layer of batting (page 38). Finish as you did the other appliqués. When the head is completed, hand-sew the white face appliqué to the grey head shape. Embroider the eyes and the nose.

For the body, first cut out the shape from the drawing, place the paper on grey fabric and draw around it. Place the grey fabric on a layer of batting and backing fabric. Sew the outline by machine. Trim the shape. Appliqué by hand the remaining small and large white appliqués to the appropriate areas. Appliqué the head in position. Hand-quilt the fine lines that appear in the illustration.

For the back of the cushion, cut on the bias (see Diagram 15, page 46) 10 inch (25 cm) wide strips from the grey fabric. Join the diagonal seams to make a 45 inch (114 cm) length. Square off each end of the strip and finish the edges on a machine. On one side of the strip length finish the edge, leaving room for a draw-string. Sew the raw edge of the other side of the strip to the front of the cushion, following the sewn outline.

To make the pillow form inside, add 1 inch (2.5 cm) all around the original drawing and transfer the shape to two layers of unbleached cotton. Sew, leaving an opening for stuffing. Put in stuffing and close the opening.

Insert the pillow form into the cushion cover, close the opening with the draw-string, and tie with a bow.

A Basket of Eggs. The finished size is approximately 13 x 14 inches (33 x 36 cm), but it can be made larger or smaller to fit the teapot.

Suggested materials. Approximately 1 yard (91 cm) of unbleached white cotton is needed for the tea-cosy form, including the lining. You will need approximately 18 inches (46 cm) square of blue fabric for cutting bias strips for the trim. Use a scrap of light brown fabric for the brown eggs. Also, you will need two squares of polyester batting 15 x 16 inches (38 x 41 cm) for padding, and blue and brown thread.

You will also need paper for the drawing, a piece of card for the egg templates, tracing or tissue paper, and a soft lead pencil or dressmaker's carbon paper. For shading, use a yellow ochre colored pencil or a liquid embroidery pen.

Method. Start by drawing the basket, referring to the illustration. Enlarge to the size you prefer. Note that the sides of the basket are only slightly curved inwards, because the teapot will fill out the shape later. Draw a few eggs on card paper (all eggs are not created equal), and cut them out for use as templates. Draw egg shapes on the drawing of the basket, overlapping until you have a realistic arrangement for your final rendering.

Make a tracing of the drawing of the basket of eggs and transfer the drawing to two pieces of white fabric, one for each side of the cosy. Transfer either with soft lead pencil or with dressmaker's carbon (page 31).

Choose a few eggs from your arrangement to be brown eggs. Make tracings of them from the original drawing. Make egg appliqués by sewing the tracing-paper patterns to two layers of brown fabric (page 35). Remove paper, trim, notch, and clip (page 34). Slit the side on which the true image appears (important for asymmetrical shapes) and turn inside out (page 35). Baste and appliqué shapes to appropriate areas on the white fabric.

Place each piece of fabric with the drawing and egg appliqués on layers of batting and backing. Baste all layers together, thoroughly (page 42). Machine-quilt all lines, with brown thread for eggs and blue for the basket. Tip: for starting and finishing thread ends, thread them through a needle, pull them to the back of the basket, and knot.

Cut from the blue fabric bias strips 1½ inches (4 cm) wide. Sew one raw edge of each strip to the inner side of each handle (as you would if you were binding it), and fold the strip outward over the edge of the handle shape. When the two sides of the tea-cosy are finally sewn together, this raw edge will be hidden in the seam. Add another strip to the top rim of the basket, raw edges turned under, and sewn in place. To do the basket rim behind the eggs, thread the needle with blue thread and hand-stitch in zig-zags, filling in between the lines as in the illustration. With a colored pencil or a liquid embroidery pen, shade a few eggs.

With the fronts of both sides of the tea-cosy facing each other, sew together, leaving the bottom open. Trim and turn right side out. To make the handle more realistic, machine-sew a line of stitching on the inside line of the blue strip. Bind the bottom opening with blue trim (page 46).

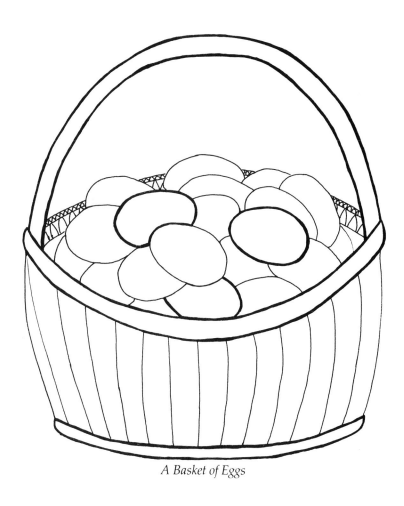

A Basket of Eggs

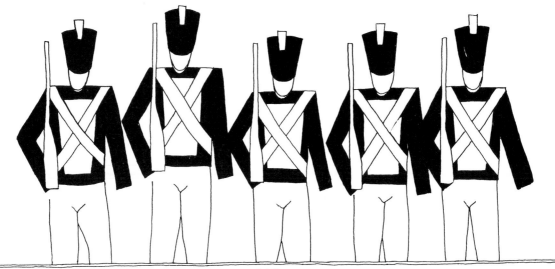

Soldiers

USING DESIGNS
FOR BORDER MOTIFS
Soldiers and Sheep

**Wall hangings, vest, and bunting
using a repeated pattern.**
Photos on pages 16 and 41.

Soldiers and *Sheep Look Up* were first done as small wall hangings. After being worked out on a small scale, they were undertaken as large pieces. Both themes succeeded as large works, and also as simple repeat motifs for practical applications such as the vest and the baby bunting pictured here. I have even drawn sheep on long strips of cloth to be quilted as bed dusters. Other suggestions for repeats are padded crib liners, window or bed valances, quilts, and almost any border designs. Keep in mind that it's the loose handling of these designs that gives them much of their individual charm.

The Soldiers. The size of the soldiers depends on the format you are working to. There is no need of a grid to enlarge this design. Just use the illustration as a guide to the proportions and positions of the elements.

Suggested materials. In the large hanging (page 41 and the back cover) brown wool fabric is used for the uniforms and for the hats; red silk for the breast pieces; red satin for the cockades; natural linen for the faces; white polished cotton for the crosses; grey-brown lining for the guns. The background and the backing are unbleached cotton with polyester batting bound in dark red broadcloth.

For the small sketch in fabric I chose brown silk uniforms and hats; grey grosgrain ribbon for guns on a background of white wool trimmed in satin cord on a foam form.

Appliqués were sewn in matching threads. The quilting in both pieces was done in black stitching.

For the blue denim bunting (page 61), the soldiers were done in navy, red, and white cotton broadcloth with cockades of red satin ribbon. The guns were made of blue grosgrain ribbon.

Method. Start by deciding the size of the format on which you wish to place the soldiers. Cut the background and lay out on a flat surface. To determine the size of the soldiers, cut card paper rectangles approximately the size you want and arrange them on the background. If necessary, adjust the sizes of the rectangles until they look right. Take one rectangle and add pieces for the details, keeping them in proportion with the illustration.

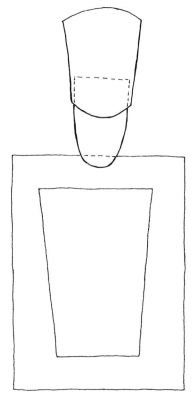

Templates for The Soldiers

than twice the length that it will actually appear on the hat. Fold the end under, place it in the upper middle of the hat, fold under the top to the appropriate length. Attach with machine sewing. Sew the bill of the hat to the face.

Arrange the bodies on the background fabric, heads slightly overlapping the tunics. Attach the arm strips to the shoulders, making a tuck on the arm that will carry the gun. Pin and baste the pieces in place. Make each gun by cutting a strip of grosgrain. Turn the raw edge under and place it where the hand holding it would be. Approximately one third of the way along the grosgrain strip start folding the ribbon inward to form the barrel of the gun. Appliqué the pieces to the background. For pants, just draw two lines extending from the sides of the tunic, a wedge, and a V for the split of the legs. Place the entire background on a layer of batting and backing, then baste. Sew lines on legs by machine. Hand or machine-quilt around the rest of the bodies.

Cut out a breast piece, cross-strips, hat, head (the head piece is the same shape as the hat only slightly smaller, and tucked under the bill of the hat), gun, and strips for arms. These pieces of card become template patterns used for tracing appliqué shapes on the fabrics.

If you are making the larger wall hanging, cut the rectangles and strips out of fabric, leaving proper seam allowances. Turn under the edges and press to prepare them for use as appliqués. For the remaining shapes (head, hat, and gun) make faced appliqués (page 35).

If you are making the smaller version, it will be easier to handle the appliqués if you face all the shapes first. Form a production line, making all the bodies, then all the chest pieces, all the heads, etc.

This is the order in which the soldiers are assembled: Sew the breast piece to the body rectangle. Sew on cross-strips one at a time, folding the ends to the back of the body. For the cockade, cut a strip of satin ribbon a little more

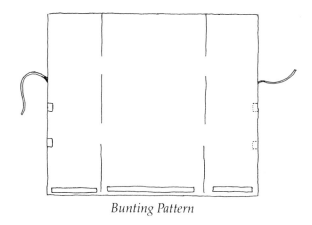

Bunting Pattern

For the *bunting bag* (page 61), cut out a piece of fabric 45 x 36 inches (114 x 91 cm). After appliquéing your design to the background, you can either add a layer of backing and batting, quilt them together, and trim; or you can leave the outer piece as it is, add trim to it and make a removable interlining. Either way, make Velcro® fastenings for the bottom and for the opening, with a red tie. This way, the bunting can be opened up and used as a blanket.

Sheep Look up
Private Collection, 22 x 33 in. (56 x 84 cm)

Sheep Look Up – *small version.* The suggested finished size of the whole piece is 22 x 33 inches (56 x 84 cm). Each square of the design illustrated here represents 1 inch (2.5 cm) in the final.

Suggested materials. The original small *Sheep Look Up* was done entirely in silk fabrics. The sky is Raja silk, the foreground and sheep a fine twill silk. I have executed this piece many times, varying the colors and textures in the materials used. For the heads, both felt and velveteen have been used; the legs and ears have been done in black embroidery floss and in couched chenille yarn. Pieces have been bound in black broadcloth and in velveteen. The backing is unbleached cotton. You will need padding for the entire piece, either polyester felt or a thin layer of batting. Batting is also used in the sheep appliqués.

You will also need paper for the sheep design, a fine-tipped felt pen and a hard lead pencil. You may need, according to the weight of fabric used, tracing or tissue paper for the pattern as well as a soft lead pencil or dressmaker's carbon.

Method. To make an appliqué of the flock of sheep, trace the sheep in the illustration, joining the lines surrounding the sheep to form a grid. On a sheet of paper, draw a grid of 1 inch (2.5 cm) squares and fill in the drawing, referring to the illustration. When this is done, fill in the background sheep freehand, as in *Sheep Look Up,* slightly reducing the size of the shapes as they recede to the horizon. If you use a lightweight white fabric for the appliqué, retrace the lines with a black felt pen and place the fabric on top of the drawing. Trace the drawing through the fabric with a hard lead pencil. Alternatively, you can use other transfer methods described earlier (page 31). In either case, do not include the legs in this appliqué; they will be added later.

To make a sewing guideline on the reverse side for facing the appliqué of the flock, place the fabric on dressmaker's carbon paper face up, or reverse the fabric and tape it to a window so that the light shines through. Retrace the top and bottom outlines of the design on the fabric. Following these lines on the reverse side of the top fabric, sew to another piece of fabric of the same size, and a final layer of batting, in one operation (page 38). Leave the sides open. Trim the batting close to the seams. Trim the shapes ⅛ inch (3 mm) from the seam, notch and clip (page 34). Use the open sides to turn inside out, push out the edges (page 34 and 35), dampen and press.

Baste the appliqué of the sheep from the center outward to prepare for quilting (page 42). For fluffy sheep, hand-quilt without a hoop on a table top. Sheep can also be machine-quilted successfully, as in the vest.

For the background, start by cutting a suitable size of both backing and padding. Decide the position of the flock of sheep and cut out appropriate sizes of fabric for the sky and the foreground. Lay the padding on top of the backing, then sky and foreground over both. Baste the appliqué of the sheep in place and slip-stitch.

To make felt heads, cut head shapes from your original drawing and use as templates with felt. Cut them out of the felt, one at a time, and sew in place on the appliqué.

To make velveteen heads, cut out triangles from the fabric, a little larger than the finished size. Start sewing each head in place by tucking under one point of the triangle. Continue

Sheep Pattern

71

to the next corner, turning the edge as you sew until the head is complete. The velveteen heads are more rounded and therefore more realistic.

For the ears and the legs, satin stitch by hand with black embroidery floss; or fold a length of chenille yarn, attach folded end and couch to the length required, secure the ends and snip off excess yarn.

Finish the piece by binding with cotton broadcloth or velveteen (page 46).

Sheep Look Up – *large version* (not shown). The finished size is 5 x 7 feet (1.5 x 2.1 m). Each square in the illustrated design therefore represents 4 inches (10 cm) in the large design. In *Sheep on a Hillside* (page 40) each square represents 6 inches (15 cm).

For fabrics in the larger renderings, heads have been made of stuffed, textured black velvet, ears and legs of black velveteen, and all were faced shaped appliqués (page 35) using black broadcloth as the facing fabric. The bodies of the sheep are made of unbleached cotton shirred and then faced (page 50). Since the backgrounds are larger, quilting is required across them to hold the layers together. Otherwise, the method remains much the same as in the smaller version.

When used as a repeat motif, as in the vest (page 73), the treatment is the same except that when transferring the design to the fabric, the pattern should be moved along, overlapping the beginning and the end of each repeat.

Vest pattern. For constructing the vest (see pattern diagram) you will need approximately 2 yards (1.8 m) for the outside fabric of the garment, plus the same again for the lining and the padding. You will also need ½ yard (46 cm) of black for the neck and the armholes. For the appliqué (three rows of sheep) you will need two lengths of fabric 40 x 6 inches (102 x 15 cm).

The appliqué is made using the same procedure as the small rendering of *Sheep Look Up*, and is applied after the vest is completed.

For the pattern of the vest, take the hip measurement, add liberal allowances for seams and body movement, and divide by two to give the width of the garment. For length, measure from the nape of the neck to the desired length, plus a hem allowance. With these measurements, make a rectangular pattern on paper (newspaper will do). Using the pattern, cut the back rectangles for the outer fabric, lining and padding. Set aside.

Divide the rectangle in half on paper, adding a few inches to one side for the front opening. Cut from paper, and discard the remaining half. Cut two pieces each of the outer fabric, lining and padding.

Assemble the three sections, placing batting between the outer layer and the lining. Taper the shoulders and cut the neck opening as illustrated in the diagram. Fold the edge of the front opening under and finish the hem. Sew the shoulders together, seams facing out. Trim and cover the seams with black fabric strips. Top-stitch in place.

For rolled neck and sleeves, cut 4 inch (10 cm) wide bias strips from the black fabric. Sew one side to the lining, insert a roll of batting, and sew the other side to the front, closing the open ends at the neck. Sew the side seams facing out, trim, and after turning the vest inside out sew the seams again.

Finish the bottom of the vest by turning the edge under and sewing. Insert a zipper or other closure at the front.

Sew the sheep to the vest by hand. Apply legs. On the two front panels, the top of the appliqué is left open to form pockets.

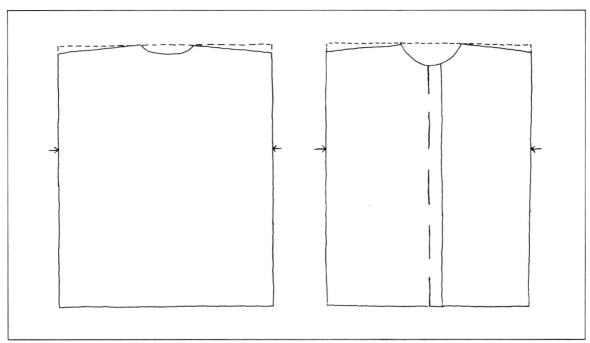

Vest Pattern, Back (left) and Front (right)

Sheep Vest, *(back)*

Sheep Vest, *(front)*

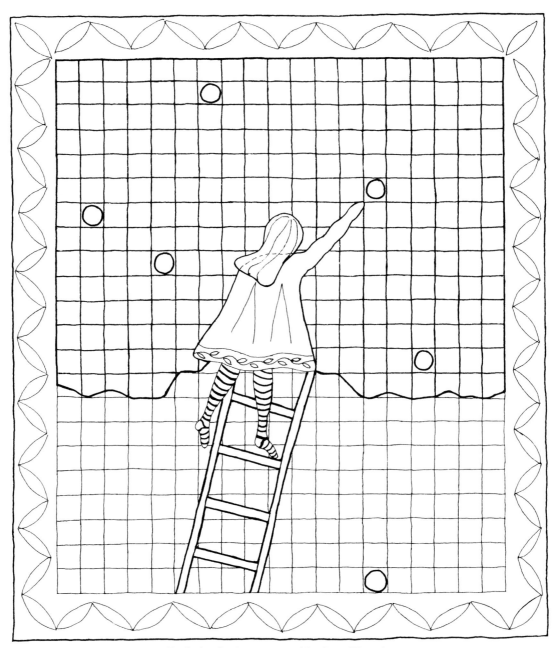

Eve's Apple, 1 square = 4 inches (10 cm)

QUILTS FOR EITHER THE BED OR THE WALL

Eve's Apple
Photo on front cover and on page 8.

Eve's Apple began life as a greeting card made for a friend. Later it occurred to me that the design was suitable for a quilt that would combine the traditions of the pieced square with regular and reverse appliqué and quilting. Being a near-novice at quilt construction at that time, I took my design to an experienced quilt-maker and admired friend, Rena Ringer. Together, we worked out the technical and design problems and set about making, entirely by hand, *Eve's Apple* – a latter-day quilt. This design, which combines a number of traditional quilt-making techniques, became my apprenticeship piece.

Eve's Apple then took on a life of its own. Entered in the Nova Scotia Designer-Craftsmen's juried show in 1976, it won the "Most Outstanding Entry" award at the Exhibition and became part of the organization's permanent collection. It has been exhibited many times since then, appeared in several magazines and in a movie, and is the cover of this book. It also brought me my first public recognition as a quiltist.

Eve's Apple. The finished size is approximately 92 x 104 inches (2.33 x 2.64 m). One square in the diagram = 4 inches (10 cm) in the finished piece.

Suggested materials. For the top white background material, use a bed sheet or sheeting of cotton or cotton-type fabric the size of the quilt. You will need the same again for the backing, or two 3 yard (2.75 m) lengths of unbleached cotton at least 48 inches (1.22 m) wide, seamed together in the middle. Also needed are 4 yards (3.65 m) of black ticking or similar stripe fabric and ¼ yard (23 cm) each of bright red and yellow broadcloth for apples and hair. To bind, use either 15 yards (14 m) of bias tape 1 inch (2.5 cm) wide or cut bias strips 1½ inches (4 cm) wide from 2 yards (1.83 m) of black broadcloth. These strips are also used in making the ladder. Pre-wash all fabrics.

You will need a piece of bonded polyester batting the size of the quilt.

For thread, use spools of white, black, red, and yellow, and skeins of yellow and black embroidery floss.

You will also need brown paper; large sheets of tracing paper (tissue will do); ruler; straight pins; masking tape; pencil; tailor's chalk or pencil; dressmaker's carbon.

Method. Make a tracing of the girl in Diagram 1 here, joining the lines on the grid surrounding the figure. On a piece of brown paper 36 x 48 inches (91 x 122 cm) draw a grid in 4 inch (10 cm) squares and fill in the drawing of the girl, referring to the tracing. When it is completed, make a tracing paper pattern of the dress and the legs with lines for quilting and embroidery. Make a tracing paper pattern for the hair as well. To make the hair appliqué, transfer the outline with dressmaker's carbon to two layers of the yellow fabric. Sew, following the outline, the two layers together. Trim the shape and notch (page 34). Cut a slit on the side in which the true image will appear and turn the shape inside out (page 35). Dampen and press (page 34 and 35).

Make the tree as follows. From the stripe fabric, measure, mark, and cut 266 squares 4½ x 4½ inches (11.5 x 11.5 cm). Make 19 strips of 14 squares each by joining them with stripes perpendicular as shown in the photograph on page 8. Stitch ¼ inch (6 mm) seams; press all seams open. Then, join strips together in ¼ inch (6 mm) seams, one by one, to form tree. Turn under the edge of the top and of the two sides ¼ inch (6 mm), and press.

Smooth out the white background fabric on the floor. Center the tree, right side up, at the upper end of the background, leaving an 8 inch (20 cm) border of white at the top and the sides; pin together. Cut the girl's shape out of the brown paper, without the hair (note dotted line in Diagram 1). Position the pattern for the girl, matching the natural grid of the tree squares to the diagram. Pin in place. Trace the outline of the girl on the tree; remove the pattern. Now, draw the uneven edge of the bottom of the tree so that it meets the hem of the girl's dress as shown in the diagram. Hand-baste ⅝ inch (15 mm) within the edges of the tree and around the outline of the girl. Leaving a ¼ inch (6 mm) seam allowance, cut out the bottom edge of the tree and the shape of the girl. *Cut only through the stripe fabric.* Turn under the uneven edge of the tree ¼ inch (6 mm); baste all edges of the tree to the white background. Slip-stitch the edges to the background. For easier quilting, cut away the excess layer of white under the tree fabric.

Now pin the hair in place with its edges overlapping the tree; baste and slip-stitch.

Replace the brown paper pattern of the girl on the tree and trace the bottom edge of the dress and the outline of the legs; remove the pattern. Take the tracing paper pattern of the girl and the legs and transfer all stitching lines to the appropriate areas. To do this, perforate the tracing paper with tailor's pencil or a tracing wheel and dressmaker's carbon, leaving a dotted line to follow on the fabric (page 31). Using black floss, embroider in chain stitch just the horizontal stocking lines on the legs. Embroider lines in the hair with yellow floss.

For marking squares to be quilted on the white background, you have a choice. Either mark the 4 inch (10 cm) squares with tailor's chalk; or, if you want to avoid marking the material, lay down guidelines with masking tape. Whichever way you choose, start at the bottom edge of the tree, continuing the vertical lines (leaving the same border width at the bottom and sides as around the tree), and then add the horizontal lines to make 4 inch (10 cm) squares.

From black bias tape, cut strips to make the ladder. Refer to Diagram 1 for ladder placement. The length of the ladder will vary slightly, depending on how you place the girl. Rungs are 10½ inches (27 cm) long. Cut strips to fit around the girl's legs; baste strips in place; appliqué.

Draw six 3¾ inch (95 mm) circles on tracing paper. To keep the shapes accurate, sew each paper pattern circle directly onto two layers of red fabric. Tear away the paper, trim the circles, and notch (page 34). Make a slit in one side and turn inside out for faced appliqué (page 35). Appliqué apples should be positioned as in Diagram 1.

Diagram 2

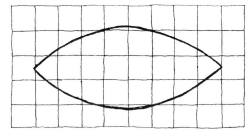

Template for Leaf Border,
1 square = 1 inch (2.5 cm)

For the quilted leaf border, make a cardboard pattern of the motif in Diagram 2. Again, you have a choice of marking-out methods: tailor's chalk, or pins placed around the template at the time of quilting, inserted at right angles to the surface line to make it easier to follow the curved line accurately. Whichever method you choose, place the pattern on the fabric border, divide it up evenly with pins first to mark where the motif ends meet, then trace around them. Notice that the motifs in the bottom corners are placed differently from those at the top.

Tape the backing material to a flat surface, seams facing up. Unroll the batting over the backing. Place the quilt top, right side up, on the batting; pin. Hand-baste all three layers together before quilting. Starting at the center of the quilt, baste out to the mid-point of each side, using a long stitch and basting through all layers. Then return to the center and baste diagonally to each corner. Finally, baste in concentric squares about 18 inches (46 cm) apart, including the outside edge. See page 42.

All the final quilting is done using white thread. If you are using a quilting hoop, start in the middle and try to work concentrically outward. Quilt the following lines: those on the girl's dress; leg outlines; ladder; squares at bottom half; leaf border. Quilt the tree squares ¼ inch (6 mm) from either side of the seamlines.

Embroider your name or the title *Eve's Apple* in the bottom corner using black floss, next to the apple, as part of the design.

Bind the edges of the quilt with black tape (page 46). Remove all basting.

The French Hen and Baby Chick
Companion bed and crib quilts

The French Hen was a wedding gift to my brother Dan and his wife Marianne. To honor the arrival of my niece, Anne, I made the *Baby Chick*. The theme of adult and infant, and the quilted egg motif, unite them as companion pieces.

The French Hen
Photo on page 81.

Finished size is 84 x 86 inches (2.11 x 2.18 m). One square on the diagram = 5 inches (127 mm) in the final piece.

Suggested materials. For the top white background, use a bed sheet or sheeting of cotton or cotton-type fabric the size of the quilt. You will need the same for the backing, or two 2½ yard (2.3 m) lengths of unbleached cotton or contrasting fabric 45 inches (114 cm) wide, seamed together in the middle. The backing is the same red and green cotton plaid as was used later on the front of the crib quilt. You will need 3 yards (2.75 m) of a printed cotton for the hen image. The comb is half a yard (46 cm) of red cotton broadcloth. Eight 1 inch wide (2.5 cm) strips are cut out of 2½ yards (2.3 m) of black cotton. These strips, with their edges turned in ¼ inch (6 mm) become the double ½ inch (12 mm) stripes for the inside border. Four 3 inch wide strips are cut for the straight edge of the binding, four bias strips for corners. Pre-wash all fabrics.

You will need a piece of bonded polyester batting the size of the quilt.

Use green, red, and black thread, with beige for quilting. Red yarn or floss is used to tie the hen to the backing.

You will need a piece of brown paper 54 x 64 inches (1.3 x 1.6 m), sheets of tracing tissue, and card paper for making templates. Also a ruler, straight pins, and tailor's chalk or pencil.

Method. Make a tracing of just the hen in Diagram 1, joining the lines bordering the illustration to make a grid. On your piece of brown paper draw a grid of 5 inch (127 mm) squares and fill in the drawing of the hen, refer-ring to the tracing. When that is completed, make a tracing-paper pattern of the comb. To make the comb appliqué, sew tissue tracing to two layers of red fabric following the drawn line on the paper. Remove the paper (page 35). Clip and notch the fabric shape, as shown in Diagram 2, page 34. Turn inside out, dampen, and press (page 34 and 35).

The French Hen

Make the hen as follows. Cut out the shape, including inside cut-outs of the head and the wing, from brown paper. Detach the head from the body along the line indicated in Diagram 1. Arrange the patterns on the printed fabric and trace the outlines of the body, head, and inside cut-outs with a white tailor's pencil. Do not trim the shapes yet. On the sewing machine, sew along the traced outline, including inside details of the wing and head cut-outs on both pieces to make a stitched guideline (page 34) on the hen appliqué. Now, trim the shapes leaving ¼ inch (6 mm) edge allowance all round, including the inside cut-outs. Notch and clip appropriately (page 34).

Smooth out the white background fabric on the floor and secure it with tape. Center the hen, right side up. Pin together. Baste the edges at least ½ inch (13 mm) inside the stitched guideline on the shapes. Slip-stitch, turning under the edges as you sew this large appliqué to the background (Diagram 3, page 34).

The French Hen, 1 square = 5 inches (13 cm)

Now pin and baste the comb in place. Appliqué to the hen.

Arrange eight ½ inch (13 mm) black stripes, referring to Diagram 1 for placement. Cut the stripes that appear to be behind the head of the hen to fit at the point where they meet the head. Pin, baste, and slip-stitch to the background.

For the quilting pattern, make a cardboard template of an egg shape. The template is placed at random, starting along the bottom and receding to the top. The pattern can be transferred by one of two methods: either by tracing around the template with a pencil until the shapes fill the area; or at the time of quilting pins can be placed at right angles to the surface of the quilt around the egg template. The template is removed, and as the quilting proceeds the pins are removed one by one. The process is repeated for each egg shape. Of the two methods, I prefer the second: it requires no pencil markings, and the shapes can be positioned more casually.

Tape the backing material to a flat surface, seams facing up. Unroll the batting over the backing. Place the quilt top, right side up, on the batting, and pin together. Hand-baste all three layers together before quilting. (See Diagram 12, page 42.)

All quilting is done using beige or light brown thread. If you are using a hoop, start in the middle and work outwards to the edge. First, instead of quilting the hen to the backing, secure it with single stitches of embroidery floss, each one tied at the front surface, leaving short ends hanging. This gives a feather-like effect. Hand-quilt around the hen outline and inside cut-out areas. Starting below the hen, quilt the egg shapes, building upwards to the top of the inside frame. Quilt lines between the inside and outside borders as indicated in Diagram 1.

Bind the straight edges of the quilt with 3 inch (76 mm) strips cut cross-grain; use bias strips at the rounded corners (page 46). Sign the quilt and remove all basting.

Note: An alternative approach, which gives quicker results, would be to machine-sew the appliqué shapes either in straight or satin stitch.

The Baby Chick

Finished size is 45 x 60 inches (114 x 152 cm). Each square in the diagram = 2.5 inches (6 cm) in the final piece.

Suggested materials. For the top yellow background use a length of cotton or cotton-like fabric 45 x 60 inches (1.14 x 1.52 m), and the same again for the backing. For the chick, you will need a 16 x 20 inch (41 x 51 cm) piece of fabric. If you are using the same print as you used in *The French Hen*, there should be enough scraps left to make the chick. For the inside border around the chick I used 4 inch (10 cm) wide strips pieced together from scraps of both the plaid and the print used in the French Hen quilt. They can also be made of solid strips cut from ½ yard (46 cm) of 45 inch (114 cm) wide fabric. The eyes and beak are scraps of white and red. For binding, you will need ¾ yard (68 cm) of black material. Pre-wash all materials.

You will also need a piece of bonded polyester batting the size of the quilt.

Use red thread for quilting and black thread for stitching. Skeins of light green and yellow were used for the eyes and the beak.

You will also need a sheet of tracing paper or tissue for the chick pattern, and cardboard for the large egg template and the corner motif. Also a ruler, straight pins, and a tailor's pencil.

Method. Draw the chick on a sheet of paper measuring at least 12 x 16 inches (30 x 41 cm). To make the faced appliqué trace your drawing to make a tissue pattern and sew, following the outline, to two layers of printed fabric. Sew the eye ovals on the print at the same time. Remove the paper. (Method on page 35.) Or you can cut out the drawing, place it on the two layers of fabric, trace around it, and then sew. When the sewing is finished and the shape trimmed and notched, cut out the two layers of fabric inside the eyes. Then cut the facing around the eye ovals and push through eye openings. Turn the piece inside out, dampen and press (page 35, 36). Make the faced beak appliqué and sew it to the face.

Smooth out the yellow background on the floor. Center the chick on the background, placing the white fabric scrap under the eye openings. Pin and baste. Arrange strips to frame the chick as shown in photo and sew where there are joins. Pin and baste the frame to the background. Slip-stitch all pieces to the yellow background. Embroider the eyes and the beak with your light green and yellow thread. Sew a tuft of red yarn to the top of the head.

To make the egg template, you will need a piece of cardboard at least 18 x 20 inches (46 x 51 cm). Enlarge and cut out. Use this pattern as described in the instructions for *The French Hen*, either drawing around it with a pencil or using it as a guide for placing pins at the time of quilting. For the corners you will need to cut templates for a small circle and for a pointed oval.

Tape the backing material to a flat surface and unroll the batting over the backing. Put down the quilt top. Pin and baste, starting in the middle (page 42).

All quilting is done in red thread. Using a quilt hoop, start in the middle and quilt concentrically outward (page 42).

Bind edges, sign, and remove all basting.

Baby Chick
1 square = 2.5 inches (6 cm)

Baby Chick
Anne Swim, 45 x 60 in. (114 x 152 cm)

The French Hen
Dan and Marianne Swim, 84 x 86 in. (213 x 218 cm)

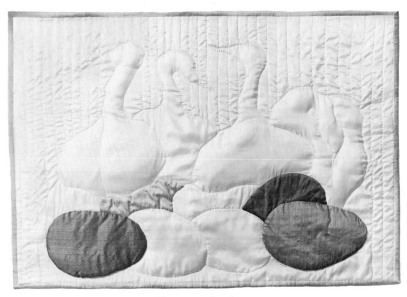

Geese a-laying
Pam Freir and Chris Bayliss, 40 x 30 in. (102 x 76 cm)

MURALS

Geese a-laying
Photo on page 82.

This simple elegant design is predominantly a hand-quilted drawing on white with a few colored eggs as accents.

Geese a-laying. The finished size is 40 x 30 inches (102 x 76 cm). One square in the illustration = 5 inches (13 cm) in the final piece.

Suggested materials. For the top white background material, use silk or other suitable fabric the size of the piece. You will need the same size of batting (double thickness) and cotton backing. For the appliqués you will need fabric in the three colors of your choice. The largest piece is 9 x 12 inches (23 x 30 cm); facing is also needed. For binding, you will need ¼ yard (23 cm) of 45 inch wide (114 cm) fabric for 1½ inch wide (3.8 cm) straight grain strips. For thread, use matching colors.

You will also need a 40 x 30 inch (102 x 76 cm) sheet of paper for drawing, and tissue or tracing paper for appliqué patterns. You may need tracing paper the size of the piece and a soft lead pencil or dressmaker's carbon if you use the tracing paper transfer method (page 31).

Method. Make a tracing of the drawing and form a grid by joining the lines surrounding the picture. On paper the size of the piece draw a grid of 5 inch (13 cm) squares and fill in the drawing. If you have chosen lightweight fabric to work with, you can use the drawing directly by placing the fabric over it and tracing the lines onto the fabric. If the fabric is too opaque to allow this, use one of the transfer methods described earlier.

Make faced appliqués from tracing paper patterns of egg-shapes. Heavy lines on the illustration indicate the appliqué shapes. Sew tracings to two layers of fabric in the colors you have chosen. Remove the paper, trim, and notch (page 34). Make a slit and turn inside out (page 35). Appliqué eggs onto the background in their proper position.

Place the background fabric with drawn lines and the appliqués on a double layer of batting and backing. Baste together (page 42). Place the piece in a hoop or stretcher (page 42). Hand-quilt lines in white on drawing, and around the appliqués.

Bind the piece using straight-grain strips (page 47) and select a method for hanging it (page 25).

Geese a-laying, 1 square = 5 inches (13 cm)

His Pride
Photos on pages 44, 86, 87.

This is a diptych, a double tablet or two separate pieces hung together as a balanced pair. The background of both pieces is the same. The tree-shapes, the lion, and the lionesses are appliquéd to the finished landscapes. The total effect is of a bas relief.

His Pride. Each half is approximately 32 x 58 inches (81 x 147 cm). One square in the diagram = 3 inches (7.5 cm).

Suggested materials. The originals were done in silk and bound in velveteen. You will need 1½ yards (1.35 m) of green for the foreground and trees, ¾ yard (69 cm) of orange for the middle ground, ½ yard (46 cm) of light yellow for the top ground, and 1 yard (91 cm) of pale pink for the sky. For the lions you will need 1 yard (91 cm) of gold fabric. You will also need scraps of hot pink and orange for tree trim and ¼ yard (23 cm) of light green for some of the trees. 1 yard (91 cm) of rust velveteen will do for the border. Add to this polyester batting and backing material the size of the pieces.

Use green, yellow, orange, and red thread.

Method. Start by making the background pieces. Cut two pieces of green fabric 24 x 36 inches (61 x 91 cm) each, two orange pieces 12 x 36 inches (30 x 91 cm) each, two pieces of yellow 9 x 36 inches (23 x 91 cm) each, and two pieces of pale pink 14 x 36 inches (36 x 91 cm) each. Take one piece from each color and sew together with ½ inch (13 mm) seam allowances in the above order. Do the same with the other set of pieces. Check to make sure that the horizontal lines of each section of the diptych line up.

To make the trees that appear on the horizon, cut two strips of paper 12 x 36 inches (30 x 91 cm) and two pieces 12 x 18 inches (30 x 46 cm). Draw tree shapes freehand approximately 9 inches (23 cm) high using the bottom edge of the paper as your horizon. Cut out and use as patterns. Cut the longer pieces from the dark green fabric and the short ones from the lighter green. Face each tree shape with the hot pink and orange scraps, leaving the bottom straight line open (page 35). Turn under the straight edge. Pin, baste, and sew the finished pieces to the horizons on the background pieces.

Transfer the quilting lines (methods on page 31) to the top pieces. Construct a fabric sandwich (page 42) with top, padding, and backing. Quilt the lines in the green foreground in red thread, orange and yellow areas in matching threads, and lines around the tree shapes with matching threads. Set these pieces aside until the lions are completed.

To make the lion and the lionesses, start by enlarging them using the grid method (page 30).

Use the tracing paper technique (page 31) to transfer the image, including inside details, to the front of the gold fabric.

To make appliqués, use faced appliqué technique (page 35), with prominent bas relief (page 38). Lioness shapes are all on one piece of fabric.

When you have completed the appliqué shapes, place them on a table top and quilt the inside details. Place the finished appliqués in their correct positions, following the design, and secure with slip-stitch sewing and quilt around shapes.

Select a binding method (page 46) and a method for hanging the piece (page 25).

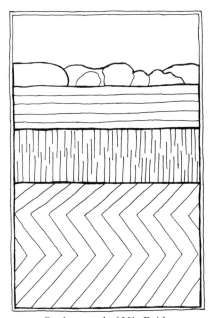

Background of His Pride

Pattern for Lion and Lionesses, 1 square = 3 inches (7.5 cm)

His Pride, *(left panel)*

His Pride, *(right panel)*

Two Crows, 1 square = 4 inches (10 cm)

Two Crows
Photo on page 56.

Two Crows creates an illusion of a window onto a country scene.

Two Crows. The finished size is 45 x 72 inches (1.14 x 1.82 m). Each square in the diagram = 4 inches (10 cm) in the final piece.

Suggested materials. This piece was completely sewn by machine. The directions are for machine sewing, although you may choose to do it by hand. Fabrics are entirely cotton. You will need 6½ yards (6 m) of white broadcloth 45 inches (114 cm) wide for the front and backing, for binding, and for the window frame. You will also need ¾ yard (69 cm) of flower print for the ground, 2 feet (61 cm) of light blue fabric for the sky, ½ yard (46 cm) of a small green print for the leaves, ¼ yard (23 cm) each of pink and brown, and a scrap of black. Batting is the size of the piece. Use matching colors of thread for everything but the lines on the wall (blue thread) and on the baseboard and floor (black thread).

Method. Enlarge the design on paper ruled in 4 inch (10 cm) squares. Each square in the design represents 4 inches (10 cm) in the enlarged drawing. Heavy lines represent appliquéd pieces. Dotted lines indicate overlapped pieces. Fine lines indicate quilting design.

Start by working on the window scene. Make tracing paper patterns of the sky and the ground material extending to the outside line of the window frame. Cut these from the blue and flower print fabrics. Fold under the top edge of the flowered piece ½ inch (13 mm) and press. Place the folded edge on the blue skypiece, pin and baste. Sew the pieces together, sewing close to the folded edge. The whole piece should be about 31 x 43½ inches (79 x 110 cm) including the allowance to be covered by the window border.

Using tracing-paper patterns, cut out leaves from the green print leaving ¼ inch (6 mm) allowance outside. Fold the edge under and straight-stitch or zig-zag in place. (For machine satin stitch see page 39.)

From the white cotton cut four strips 2½ x 43½ inches (6 x 110 cm) on length-wise grain of fabric. Fold the long edges in ½ inch (13 mm) to form 1½ inch (3.8 cm) wide pieces. Press. Place strips on each side of the ground piece, lining them up with the outer edges. Pin and baste along the outer edges of the strip; straight-stitch along the inner edges, ⅛ inch (3 mm) from the fold. Place the remaining two strips vertically so that the piece is divided into three equal sections; stitch along both long edges of each strip.

Cut another five strips 2½ x 31 inches (6 x 79 cm). Fold and press as before. Using what you have already done, and referring to the illustration, mark notches and pointed ends where needed. Make a straight cut into the notch and fold under at an angle to fit width of 1½ inches (3.8 cm) (page 88). Press. Sew five strips horizontally across the ground piece in the same manner as before, dividing it into four equal sections and crossing the vertical strips. Fold in the inner corners where they cross to give a mitered effect.

Cut two birds from your scrap of black and appliqué them to the upper left windowpane in the same way as you did the leaves. Place the tracing paper pattern of the upper portion of the woman's figure, without the head, on the window appliqué piece. Pin and baste the paper to the piece. Sew, following the outline of the figure, without the hair. Remove the paper and cut inside the figure ¼ inch (6 mm) from the marked line. Turn ¼ inch (6 mm) to the wrong side, clipping curves where necessary; press and baste.

From the remaining white cotton fabric cut background 45 x 72 inches (1.14 x 1.82 m). Position the window with figure cut-out as indicated in the design, pin and baste. Straight-stitch around the outer edges of the window, continuing stitching around the cut-out figure.

Cut two identical hairpieces, two sashes, and two bows from fabrics in colors of your choice, transferring pattern lines (page 31). Face the appliqués (page 35) with right sides facing, plus a layer of batting. Slit and turn inside out. Quilt pattern lines of hair and bow, then sew the bow to the hair. Position hair and sash appliqués on figure. Straight-stitch all around, close to the edge.

Transfer quilting lines to the white area of the quilt top (page 31). Assemble the textile sandwich (page 42). Baste for quilting (page 42). To quilt on a sewing machine, start in the center of the hanging and work outward in as circular a fashion as possible to prevent the fabric from bunching (page 43). When quilting parallel lines in blue thread on the wall, alternate the direction of the stitching between rows. Use black thread for the lines of the baseboard and the floor. Quilt around all appliqués in appropriate colors. Bind (page 46), and choose a method for hanging (page 25).

Sugar Plum, 1 square = 3 inches (7.5 cm)

Sugar Plum
Photo on title page and page 92.

Sugar Plum was originally an 8½ x 10 inch (22 x 25 cm) sketch of my young friend Rachel Goldstein. I enlarged it for this wall hanging.

Sugar Plum. The finished size is 29 x 39 inches (74 x 99 cm). One square in the diagram = 3 inches (7.6 cm) in the final piece.

Suggested materials. For the top blue background material, use cotton fabric 30 x 40 inches (76 x 102 cm). You will need the same sizes of batting and backing. For hair, you will need two pieces of brown fabric 12 x 9 inches (30 x 23 cm); for flesh, a half yard (46 cm) of rayon or silk; for the dress, a 20 x 22 inch (51 x 56 cm) piece of organza; for the border of the oval you will need 3¼ yards (3 m) of satin cord or similar; for the trim around the edge, 4 yards (3.7 m) of cord or piping. You will also need a ¾ inch thick (19 mm) slab of foam cut to the size of the piece to give it firmness (page 27).

Use matching colors of thread and blue embroidery floss.

You will also need paper 30 x 40 inches (76 x 102 cm), tracing or tissue paper for the patterns, and lead and dressmaker's pencils.

Method. Make a tracing of the girl in the diagram, then join the lines surrounding the figure to form a grid on your tracing. On your large sheet of paper draw a grid of 3 inch (8 cm) squares. Enlarge the drawing.

Pin the organza over the dress area (including the shoulder straps) on your drawing. Trace all the lines of the dress onto the organza. These will be your guidelines for quilting.

Place a sheet of tracing or tissue paper on top of the organza and the drawing. Baste the tracing paper to the perimeter of the organza only. Trace just the outline of the dress shape and remove the tracing, with the organza attached, from the drawing. Place the tracing and organza on top of the blue background fabric, with the dress in the correct position. Pin, baste, and machine-sew following the outline

of the shape on the tracing. Remove the paper (page 35). The dress fabric is now secured. Trim the organza carefully from outside the dress shape leaving a raw edge, with the exception of the area where the girl's back meets the top of the dress and the shoulder straps. Check the dotted line in the illustration. The back and shoulder are faced appliqués which will later overlap and define this area. Check the broken line in the illustration for reference to complete the appliqué shapes.

Place the blue background fabric, with the organza attached, to a layer of batting and backing. Baste (page 42). Sew another line of stitching (this can be satin-stitched by machine) following the previous outline. Machine-quilt the bottom skirt lines, the top of the skirt, and the sides of the torso to outline the shape of the upper body. Hand-quilt the remaining lines from waist to hem of the skirt. Embroider lines at the bottom of the skirt with a chain stitch if you haven't already done it in satin stitch.

From the drawing, make tracing patterns for the leg, arm/shoulder, and back areas. All these are faced appliqués; the broken lines under the hair indicate appliqué shapes. Sew tracings to two layers of flesh colored fabric. Remove the paper, trim and clip. Make slits on the side on which the true image appears and turn inside out. Baste and sew in place. Quilt the bends in the leg and the arm.

Make a tracing of the hair and sew it to two layers of brown fabric with a bottom layer of batting (Accentuated Bas Relief, page 38). Finish in the same way as the previous body appliqués. Draw lines for the hair and quilt them. Baste and sew in place.

Take the trim for the oval and place it around the figure. You may want to cut the oval shape from your working drawing and use it as a guide. Baste and sew in place, and quilt a line along side of it. Finish by placing a bow made of the trim over the join. Finishing with a foam form is described in Chapter Three (page 27). Hanging of pieces using foam is described on page 27 as well.

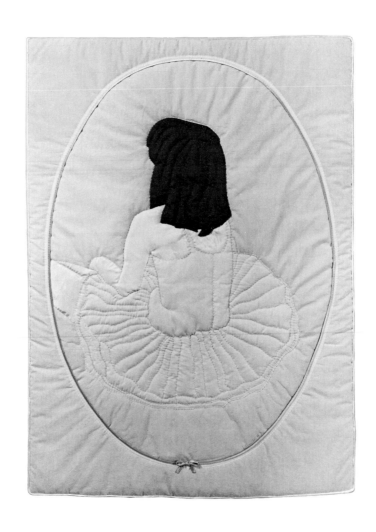

Sugar Plum
The Artist, 29 x 34 in. (74 x 86 cm)

List of Works

Index